NATIONWIDE REAL ESTATE PRE-LICENSING COURSE

Oklahoma-specific portion written for the 90-hour Oklahoma Salesperson's Real Estate Pre-licensing Course

Specializing in Oklahoma

to be taken in conjunction with:

JOSEPH R. FITZPATRICK

Real estate licensing courses and textbooks available through RealtySchool.com:

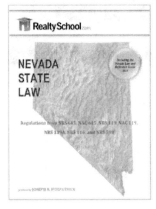

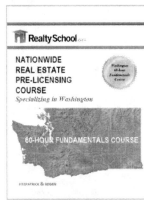

REALTYSCHOOL.COM NATIOWIDE REAL ESTATE PRE-LICENSING COURSE: *Specializing in Oklahoma*

Authored by Joseph R. Fitzpatrick
Contributing authors: Michael G. Beckner, J.D., and David Crowell
Edited by Terrance M. Fitzpatrick, Leslie Wood, and Charlotte Bentley

Third Edition 2014   021015JF
ISBN-13: 978-1495396625
ISBN-10: 1495396622

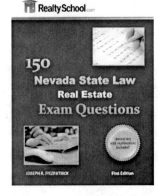

TABLE OF CONTENTS

Chapter 1

Laws and Rules Affecting Oklahoma Real Estate Practice

This chapter focuses on obtaining your Oklahoma real estate license by walking you through all the steps, from completing an Oklahoma approved pre-licensing course, all the way through receiving your license. The chapter continues with a review of ongoing education and renewal requirements in maintaining your license.

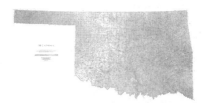

DO YOU KNOW???

Have you been acquainted with the specific powers and duties of the Oklahoma Real Estate Commission?

Do you know the requirements for licensing?

Are you familiar with how and when real estate licenses in Oklahoma are renewed?

Do you know the restrictions on advertising so your ads remain in compliance?

Have you reviewed activities that could get you in hot water with the Commission and do you know the possible penalties?

These are just some of the topics to be covered in this chapter.

THE OKLAHOMA REAL ESTATE LICENSE CODE

In 2013, the Oklahoma real estate license code was amended. The "code," section §858, is adopted and issued by the Oklahoma Real Estate Commission, the real estate licensing authority in the state. The §858-101 and 102 begin the text with definitions to be used throughout the licensing code. This author is often asked, "Am I expected to memorize *all* of these state laws for test purposes?" My response is always, "No, however. Anything within a state's licensing code is 'fair game' for a state licensing exam however we will make every effort to emphasize what we believe will be most likely tested based on our experience." We not only draw your attention to the selected laws for test purposes, but also highlight how these laws will come into play in your everyday real estate practices.

Interwoven within these chapters are Oklahoma Real Estate Commission rules (as of November 1, 2013) contained within title 605.

Students of this course may find it helpful to read the actual license law itself for better clarification. The code can be found at the Commission's web site: http://www.ok.gov/OREC/.

THE OKLAHOMA REAL ESTATE COMMISSION

The fundamental and primary purpose of the Real Estate
Commission is to safeguard the public interest and provide quality services by assisting and providing resources; encouraging and requiring high standards of knowledge and ethical practices of licensees; investigating and sanctioning licensed activities; and through the prosecution of any

unlicensed person who violates the Oklahoma Real Estate License Code and Rules. Any person may petition the Commission in writing requesting a promulgation, amendment or repeal of any rule.

The 200s section of the Code starts the chapter with the details regarding the Oklahoma Real Estate Commission. The Commission has the sole authority to issue real estate licenses in the state and regulate the practices of licensees. The Commission consists of seven (7) members. The commissioners must all be U.S. citizens and have been Oklahoma residents the prior three (3) years prior to appointment. Five (5) of the seven members must be real estate *brokers* with at least five (5) years of active, full-time, experience as a real estate broker. One (1) member must be a lay person with no real estate experience. One (1) member must be an active representative of an approved, Oklahoma real estate school located within the state. No more than two (2) members may be from the same congressional district.

Members of the Commission are appointed by the governor and confirmed through the senate. Commissioners serve a four (4) year term. The Oklahoma Association of REALTORS® provides the governor with recommendations for persons to serve. The governor can replace a commission member for failure to perform the duties required and also has the authority to fill a vacancy.

Each year, the members elect a chairperson and vice-chairperson. These two members shall attend every Commission meeting and employ a secretary-treasurer to keep minutes of the meetings. The Commission has the authority to hire administrative staff to carry out the duties as created in the license code. The commissioners also oversee all monies in the *Oklahoma Real Estate Commission Revolving Fund.* This fund contains monies collected from application and renewal fees, fines, etc., (all funds other than those collected for the *Oklahoma Real Estate Education and Recovery Fund*) and these funds may be invested at the discretion of the commissioners in securities through the *Oklahoma State Treasurer's Cash Management Program.* Commissioners have the authority to appropriate and expend funds as necessary to carry out the duties of the Commission.

The Commission has adopted a seal which is affixed to all Oklahoma real estate licenses and other commission related documents. The commission is located in Oklahoma City.

Section 858-208 lists the specific powers and duties of the Commission which are:

1. to promulgate rules, prescribe administrative fees by rule, and make orders as it may deem necessary or expedient in the performance of its duties;
2. to administer examinations to persons who apply for the issuance of licenses;
3. to sell to other entities or governmental bodies, not limited to the State of Oklahoma, computer testing and license applications to recover expended research and development costs;
4. to issue licenses in the form the Commission may prescribe to persons who have passed examinations or who otherwise are entitled to such licenses;

5. to issue licenses to and regulate the activities of real estate brokers, provisional sales associates, sales associates, branch offices, nonresidents, associations, corporations, and partnerships;

6. Upon showing good cause as provided for in The Oklahoma Real Estate License Code, to discipline licensees, instructors and real estate school entities by:
   a. reprimand,
   b. probation for a specified period of time,
   c. required education in addition to the educational requirements provided by Section 858-307.2 of this title,
   d. suspending real estate licenses and approvals for specified periods of time,
   e. revoking real estate licenses and approvals,
   f. imposing administrative fines pursuant to Section 858-402 this title, or
   g. any combination of discipline as provided by subparagraphs a through f of this paragraph;

7. Upon showing good cause, to modify any sanction imposed pursuant to the provisions of this section and to reinstate licenses;

8. to conduct, for cause disciplinary proceedings;

9. to prescribe penalties as it may deem proper to be assessed against licensees for the failure to pay the license renewal fees as provided for in this Code;

10. to initiate the prosecution of any person who violates any of the provisions of this Code;

11. to approve instructors and organizations offering courses of study in real estate and to further require them to meet standards to remain qualified as is necessary for the administration of this Code;

12. to contract with attorneys and other professionals to carry out the functions and purposes of this Code;

13. to apply for injunctions and restraining orders for violations of the Code or the rules of the Commission;

14. to create an Oklahoma Real Estate Contract Form Committee by rule that will be required to draft and revise real estate purchase and/or lease contracts and any related addenda for voluntary use by real estate licensees.

15. to enter into contracts and agreements for the payment of food and other reasonable expenses as authorized in the State Travel Reimbursement Act necessary to host, conduct, or participate in meetings or training sessions as is reasonable for the administration of this Code; and

16. To conduct an annual performance review of the Executive Director and submit the report to the Legislature; and

17. to enter into reciprocal agreements with other real estate licensing regulatory jurisdictions with equivalent licensing, education and examination requirements.

In essence, the Commission adopts rules, issues and denies licenses, regulates and disciplines licensees, and prescribes penalties for violations of the license law.

Another function of the Oklahoma Real Estate Commission is to draft and revise real estate purchase and/or lease contracts and any related addenda for standardization and use by real estate licensees. 605:1-1-4 goes into greater detail as to the rules associated with the committee charged with the responsibilities of this task.

LICENSING REQUIREMENTS

The 300s address the need for a real estate license and the requirements to receive one. 301 states, "It shall be unlawful for any person to act as a real estate licensee, or to hold himself or herself out as such, unless the person shall have been licensed to do so under this Code." Most states identify the *services of real estate* as being advertise, appraise, auction, buy, exchange, lease, rent, and sell. Some schools teach the acronym **"A BAR SALE"** to remember all eight services. The rule is: any person (or business entity), who performs *any* of these eight services of real estate, for another person, for compensation, or the expectation of compensation, is required to have a real estate license. A person who is *not* licensed and performs these duties for compensation may be sanctioned.

An additional point is to define "compensation." Compensation is defined as *anything* of value. It normally refers to money, but may be anything given in exchange for services, anything worth valuable consideration.

As with most all states, the Oklahoma code specifies those persons or entities who are exempt from needing a real estate license. Those exemptions include:

These individuals are EXEMPT from the requirement to hold a valid real estate license.

- persons with an interest in a business entity performing real estate activities for its own use
- persons acting as the attorney-in-fact for the owner of any real estate *authorizing the final consummation* by performance of any contract for the sale, lease or exchange of such real estate (can only sign contracts and closing documents).
- any attorney-at-law performing the duties of the attorney as such (can act as an attorney in a real estate transaction for a client; e.g. review contracts, but cannot act as a real estate licensee).
- a receiver, trustee in bankruptcy, administrator, executor, or his or her attorney, in performing his or her duties
- any person performing any acts under the order of any court, or acting as a trustee under the terms of any trust, will agreement or deed of trust
- any person acting as the resident manager for the owner or an employee acting as the resident manager

- any person who engages in such activity in connection with the acquisition of real estate on behalf of an entity, public or private, which has the right to acquire the real estate by eminent domain
- any person who is a resident of an apartment building, duplex, or apartment complex or court,
- when the person receives a resident referral fee not to exceed $100.00 offered to a resident for the act of recommending the property for lease
- any person or entity managing a transient lodging facility
- employees of a licensed real estate broker who leases residential housing units only to eligible
- persons who qualify through a state or federal housing subsidized program

Requirements for licensing: salespersons

Every applicant for an Oklahoma real estate license shall be required to demonstrate he is:

A. a person of good moral character (this is done through a criminal history record, background check, and required disclosures of offenses; and
B. eighteen (18) years of age or older; and
C. successfully completed ninety (90) clock hours or its equivalent of basic real estate instruction in a course of study approved by the Commission. The certificate of completion from the school is valid for three (3) years. A certified transcript from an institution of higher education certifying successful completion of a six-academic-hour basic course of real estate instruction or its equivalent, for which college credit was given, shall serve as successful completion of the clock hours as required.

Applicants may apply to the Commission to take the examination for the purpose of securing a license as a *provisional sales associate*. Applications are made using forms prescribed by the Commission, accompanied by any required documentation, and the payment of the exam fee. After passing the exam, the applicant will receive a final approval of the application and must pay the license fee along with the *Oklahoma Real Estate Education and Recovery Fund* fee. Following the issuance of a provisional sales associate license, a licensee must submit to the Commission evidence of successful completion of forty-five (45) clock hours or its equivalent, prior to the expiration of the provisional license, representing *post-license education* real estate instruction. The provisional license is good for 12 months. A certified transcript from an institution of higher education certifying successful completion of a three-academic-hour course of real estate instruction, or its equivalent, consisting of the provisional sales associate post-license education requirements for which college credit was given, shall satisfy the clock hour requirement of real estate instruction for the post-license education requirement.

Requirements for licensing: brokers and broker-associates

The Oklahoma requirements for licensure as a broker or broker-associate are slightly different:

A. two (2) years' experience, within the previous five (5) years, as a licensed real estate sales associate or provisional sales associate, or its equivalent; and

B. successful completion of ninety (90) clock hours or its equivalent of advanced real estate instruction in a course of study approved by the Commission, in addition to any instruction required for securing a license as a real estate sales associate

After the issuance of a license as a broker or broker-Associate, the licensee must successfully complete an additional ninety (90) clock hours or its equivalent in basic real estate instruction. A certified transcript from an institution of higher education certifying the successful completion of a six-academic-hours advanced course of real estate instruction, or its equivalent, for which college credit was given, shall satisfy this requirement of clock hours of advanced real estate instruction, or its equivalent.

Licensing of business entities – The Commission will also license a business entity such as a partnership, limited liability company, or corporation, as long as the managing member or broker is licensed as a real estate broker.

Non-residents – A non-resident of Oklahoma may obtain an Oklahoma non-resident license by successfully completing the Oklahoma state portion of the real estate examination. Further, the non-resident must give written consent that actions and suits at law may be commenced against the licensee in any county in the state where any cause of action may arise from a transaction occurring in the county because of the licensee's conduct. The non-resident must appoint the secretary-treasurer of the Commission as service agent to receive service of summons. Service upon the secretary-treasurer is sufficient to give the court jurisdiction over the nonresident in all such actions.

The Commission may enter into a nonresident agreement with another jurisdiction and thereby qualify *actively licensed nonresident applicants* for licensing provided the Commission determines that the educational and experience requirements of the other jurisdiction are equivalent or equal.

A non-resident applicant who holds an *inactive license* in another jurisdiction may apply to the Commission for a license to operate as a non-resident provisional sales associate or broker by submitting all appropriate documents and successfully completing all requirements as required by the Commission.

A broker who is duly licensed in another state and who has not obtained an Oklahoma non-resident license may enter a *cooperative brokerage agreement* with an Oklahoma licensed real estate broker. However, if the broker desires to perform licensed activities in this state, the broker must obtain an Oklahoma non-resident license.

605:10-7-10 explains the parameter by which an Oklahoma resident, who is currently or was previously licensed in another state, may make application for an Oklahoma license with lesser requirements than a new applicant.

Application for license after a revocation – An applicant who wishes to reapply for licensure who previously had a license revoked may not reapply within the first three years after the effective date of the revocation. The Commission maintains a list of licensees who have been suspended or revoked and makes that information a matter of public record. See more about "reinstatement" to follow.

EDUCATIONAL REQUIREMENTS FOR LICENSING

This section was taken from 605:10, subchapter 3.

Applicants for a provisional salesperson license must show evidence of having successfully completed a ninety (90) clock hours course of instruction or its equivalent as determined by the Commission. The pre-license course of study is referred to as the *Basic Course of Real Estate, Part I of II* and shall encompass the following areas of study:

(A)	Real Estate Economics and Marketing
(B)	Nature of Real Estate
(C)	Rights and Interest in Real Estate
(D)	Legal Descriptions
(E)	Title Search, Encumbrances, and Land Use Control
(F)	Transfer of Rights
(G)	Service Contracts
(H)	Estimating Transaction Expenses
(I)	Value and Appraisal
(J)	Marketing Activities
(K)	Fair Housing
(L)	Contract Law Overview
(M)	Contract Law and Performance
(N)	Offers and Purchase Contracts
(O)	Financing Real Estate
(P)	Closing a Transaction
(Q)	Regulations Affecting Real Estate
(R)	Disclosures and Environmental Issues
(S)	Property Management and Leasing
(T)	Risk Management
(U)	Professional Standards of Conduct
(V)	Law of Agency

Broker candidates must complete a ninety (90) clock hours course of instruction or its equivalent as determined by the Commission referred to as the *Advanced Course in Real Estate* and shall encompass the following areas of study:

(A)   Laws and Rules Affecting Real Estate Practice
(B)   Broker Supervision
(C)   Establishing a Real Estate Office
(D)   Professional Development
(E)   Business, Financial, and Brokerage Management
(F)   Oklahoma Broker Relationships
(G)   Anti-Trust and Deceptive Trade
(H)   Risk Management and Insurance
(I)   Mandated Disclosures, Hazards, and Zoning
(J)   Real Estate Financing
(K)   Specialized Property Operations and Specialty Areas
(L)   Trust Accounts and Trust Funds
(M)   Closing a Real Estate Transaction
(N)   Closing Statements
(O)   Professional Standards of Conduct
(P)   Property Ownership
(Q)   Land Use Controls and Regulations
(R)   Valuation and Market Analysis
(S)   Law of Agency
(T)   Contracts
(U)   Transfer of Property
(V)   Practice of Real Estate
(W)   Real Estate Calculations

Examination information – Oklahoma has contracted with PSI testing services for the administration of the state exam. PSI is a company whose services are utilized in a number of states and there are several textbooks available for purchase on how to best prepare for a PSI administered exam. Additionally, PSI has produced a *Real Estate Licensure Applicant Information Bulletin* which is a *must read* including how the computerized test works, an outline of testing content broken down by the number of questions dedicated to each topic, and how to schedule the exam. Be sure to find the Oklahoma bulletin by visiting www.psiexams.com.

Candidates who do not pass the exam may retake subsequent exams upon the payment of the required fees. An applicant who fails the examination has the option of reviewing their missed questions at the end of their examination. Applicants may challenge the validity of any questions believed incorrectly graded.

A passing score of 75% is required and passing results are good for one year.

LICENSE APPLICATIONS: APPROVAL OR DENIAL

The license application – 605:10-3-2, as well as the application form itself, clearly spells out the information required for completing the licensing application.

Applications are presented to the Commission for approval or denial. An applicant who is denied a license is entitled to a hearing according to the parameters defined within 605:10-3-3.

LICENSE RENEWAL

The term of the provisional salesperson license is twelve (12) months while the term for all other licenses is 36 months. Licenses expire on the last day of the month.

At the end of the license term, licensees who wish to remain active must renew their licenses with the real estate commission show evidence of having completed the continuing educational requirement. This requirement is not applicable to:

- licensees on inactive status (must still pay any fees required);
- licensees holding a provisional sales associate license;
- nonresident licensees if the licensee maintains a current license in another state and has satisfied the continuing education requirement for license renewal in that state

Provisional salespersons must complete an approved post-licensing course consisting of at least 45 clock hours called the Provisional Post-license Course of Real Estate, Part II of II, and shall encompass the following areas of study:

    (1) Real Estate Marketplace
    (2) Marketing Real Estate
    (3) Personal Marketing
    (4) The Qualifying Process
    (5) Prospecting and Negotiating
    (6) Financing Real Estate, Investments and Exchanges
    (7) Financial Documents
    (8) Duty to Account
    (9) Title Search
    (10) Risk Management
    (11) Broker Relationships with Parties to a Transaction
    (12) Property Management
    (13) Laws and Regulations Affecting Real Estate Practice
    (14) Disciplinary Action
    (15) Contracts

This post-licensing requirement must be completed and reported to the Commission before the end of the one year provisional license. Failure to do so will prevent the licensee from renewing and permitted to practice.

The continuing education requirement for **salespersons** is a minimum of 21 hours of Commission approved courses before the end of the three year license expiration. Oklahoma has approved both classroom as well as distance education courses. 12 of the 21 hours are mandated by the Commission:

- Professional Conduct
- Broker Relationships Act
- Fair Housing
- Current Issues including Code and Rule Updates

The remaining nine hours may be in any Commission-approved continuing education course.

Brokers must complete the 15 hour "Broker in Charge" course plus two of the four mandated topics from above.

The fees for original license applications and for renewals are listed in 605:10-7-2.

REINSTATEMENT OF LICENSE

A licensee who has not renewed a license prior to its expiration will have a license that has lapsed. In order to continue to practice real estate, the licensee, at this point, would have to apply for a reinstatement of license. The licensee will have to make payment of an amount equal to the current examination fee in addition to the license and late penalty fees for each delinquent license period. The following documents and fees must be submitted:

(1) In the case of a license lapsed less than one year:
   (A) License and late penalty fee.
   (B) Reinstatement fee.
   (C) National criminal history check.
   (D) Documents as required by the Commission.

(2) In the case of a license lapsed more than one year but less than three years:
   (A) License and late penalty fee.
   (B) Reinstatement fee.
   (C) National criminal history check.
   (D) A completed reinstatement application.
   (E) Successful completion of the appropriate licensing examination.

(F) A statement that the applicant has read a current License Code and Rules booklet.
(G) Documents as required by the Commission.

(3) If an application is submitted more than three (3) years subsequent to the most recent year of licensure, the applicant shall be regarded as an original applicant.

If the licensee is a provisional sales associate, who *did not* renew on time, but *did* complete the post-license education prior to license expiration date, the licensee can reinstate the license as a sales associate. If the education was not completed prior to the expiration date, must apply and qualify as an original applicant.

Another situation in which a licensee would apply to reinstate is in the event of electing to reinstate a revoked Oklahoma license. Applicants may not apply for a reinstatement of license for a minimum of three (3) years from the effective date of license revocation. After the three year period, the applicant shall be required to comply with the requirements of an original applicant.

An applicant who has had their license automatically revoked, pursuant to Section 858-402 or 858-604 of Title 59 of the Oklahoma Statutes, shall be required to comply with these same requirements and, in addition, must satisfy all outstanding amounts due the Commission.

A surrendered or cancelled license applicant may be reinstated provided the applicant has received approval for re-issuance from the Commission and submits the following:

(1) A surrendered or cancelled license applicant whose license term is still current:
   (A) Applicable reinstatement fee equal to the current examination fee.
   (B) Re-issuance fee equal to the transfer of license fee.
   (C) Documents as required by the Commission.
   (D) Criminal history background check.

(2) A surrendered or cancelled license applicant whose license term has expired shall be required to comply with the same requirements as the reinstatement requirements listed above depending on how long the license was surrendered or cancelled.

(3) A surrendered or cancelled provisional sales associate whose license term has expired shall be required to comply with the following:
   (A) If a provisional sales associate completed the post-license requirement on or before the first license expiration date, the applicant shall be eligible to reinstate the license according to 605:10-7-2 (f), (1) through (3).
   (B) If a provisional sales associate did not complete the post-license requirement on or before the first license expiration date, the applicant shall be required to apply and qualify as an original applicant.

MISCELLANEOUS LICENSING MATTERS – TEN DAY RULES

Since the code does not specify, it is presumed that "days" is the same as "calendar days."

A name change of a licensee or business entity must be filed with the Commission within ten (10) days of occurrence.

Any change of business address or office telephone number of a broker must be filed in the Commission office within ten (10) days of such change. A broker is required to notify the Commission of his or her current home address. Such change shall be filed in the Commission office within ten (10) days of such change.

Associates must notify the Commission within ten (10) days of a change in home address.
The licenses of every sales associate are issued to and maintained by the broker. Should an associate wish to terminate the relationship with the broker, the broker must return the license to the Commission along with the required release form. This is the same process as an associate who wishes to leave one branch and transfer to another within the same company. The filing with the Commission must be done within ten (10 days) of the occurrence. The associate may continue to perform real estate services provided the change is filed within the ten days.

In the event a broker refuses to release an associate, the associate is required to notify the broker by certified mail of the disassociation and furnish the Commission a sworn statement that the notification has been sent to the broker. Upon receipt by the Commission, the Commission shall release the licensee.

ADVERTISING RULES

605:10-9-4 begins the section on advertising requirements of Oklahoma licensees. Note that even if the broker has not seen or approved an ad run by an associate, the broker is ultimately held responsible for its compliance. A summary of advertising rules includes:

- Advertising must use the business name as licensed with the Commission.
- Yard signs must also include the broker's office telephone number.
- The name of another licensed firm may not be used.
- Advertisements must indicate that the party is a real estate broker and not a private party, to include, but not limited to, "agency", "company", "realty", or "real estate", as the case may be.
- Franchises must use the franchise name along with the name of the broker or business trade name as registered with the Commission. Advertising shall indicate that each office is independently owned and operated.
- Advertising must not be directed at or refer to persons of a particular race, color, creed, religion, national origin, familial status or handicap.

- Advertising must be confined to information relative to the property itself and discriminatory advertising is prohibited.
- Advertising must not be misleading or inaccurate in any material fact or in any way.
- The broker must first secure the permission of the owner to advertise a property.
- A licensee who is engaged in licensed activities through social networking mediums must indicate their license status and include their broker's reference as required elsewhere.
- A licensee shall not use a yard sign at the licensee's personal residence as a marketing tool, to make it appear the real property is for sale, lease or rent when such is not the case.
- Seller incentives may be advertised with the consent of the seller provided the incentive is being offered by the seller and not by the licensee and that the promotion only applies to a seller's particular property or properties.

Regarding advertising placed by associates, these are some of the more pertinent rules:

- An associate is prohibited from advertising under only the associate's name.
- All advertising by an associate must be under the direct supervision of the associate's broker.
- Associates must include the name of the associate's broker or the name under which the broker operates, in such a way that the broker's reference is prominent, conspicuous and easily identifiable.
- Open house or directional signs used in conjunction with broker's signs do not have to contain the name or trade name of the associate's broker and broker's telephone number.

When a licensee, either active or inactive, is purchasing real estate or is the owner of property that is being sold, exchanged, rented or leased and such is being handled either by the licensee or marketed through a real estate firm, the licensee is required to disclose in writing on all documents that pertain to the transaction and in all advertisements that he or she is licensed. On all purchase or lease contracts the licensee is to include their license number. A licensee who is not acting in the capacity of a licensee but is engaged in buying, selling, leasing or renting real estate as a direct employee for the owner or as an officer for an entity is not required to indicate in the advertising that he or she is licensed.

DISCIPLINARY ACTIONS

Should an aggrieved person file a written complaint to the Commission, the Commission will investigate the business transactions of the real estate licensee, and may, upon showing good cause, impose sanctions. Section 858-208 lists the acts for which a licensee may be disciplined:

1. Making a materially false or fraudulent statement in an application for a license;
2. Making substantial misrepresentations or false promises in the conduct of business, or through real estate licensees, or advertising, which are intended to influence, persuade, or induce others;
3. Failing to comply with the requirements of Sections 858-351 through 858-363 of this title;
4. Accepting a commission or other valuable consideration as a real estate associate for the performance of any acts as an associate, except from the real estate broker with whom the associate is associated;
5. Representing or attempting to represent a real estate broker other than the broker with whom the associate is associated without the express knowledge and consent of the broker with whom the associate is associated;
6. Failing, within reasonable time, to account for or to remit any monies, documents, or other property coming into possession of the licensee which belong to others;
7. Paying a commission or valuable consideration to any person for acts or services performed in violation of the Oklahoma Real Estate License Code;
8. Any other conduct which constitutes untrustworthy, improper, fraudulent, or dishonest dealings;
9. Disregard or violating any provision of the Oklahoma Real Estate License Code or rules promulgated by the Commission;
10. Guaranteeing or having authorized or permitted any real estate licensee to guarantee future profits which may result from the resale of real estate;
11. Advertising or offering for sale, rent or lease any real estate, or placing a sign on any real estate offering it for sale, rent or lease without the consent of the owner or the owner's authorized representative;
12. Soliciting, selling, or offering for sale real estate by offering "free lots," conducting lotteries or contests, or offering prizes for the purpose of influencing a purchaser or prospective purchaser of real estate;
13. Accepting employment or compensation for appraising real estate contingent upon the reporting of a predetermined value or issuing any appraisal report on real estate in which the licensee has an interest unless the licensee's interest is disclosed in the report. All appraisals shall be in compliance with the Oklahoma real estate appraisal law, and the person performing the appraisal or report shall disclose to the employer whether the person performing the appraisal or report is licensed or certified by the Oklahoma Real Estate Appraiser Board;
14. Paying a commission or any other valuable consideration to any person for performing the services of a real estate licensee as defined in the Oklahoma Real Estate License Code who has not first secured a real estate license pursuant to the Oklahoma Real Estate License Code;
15. Unworthiness to act as a real estate licensee, whether of the same or of a different character as specified in this section, or because the real estate licensee has been convicted of, or pleaded guilty or nolo contendere to, a crime involving moral turpitude;

16. Commingling with the licensee's own money or property the money or property of others which is received and held by the licensee, unless the money or property of others is received by the licensee and held in an escrow account that contains only money or property of others;

17. Conviction in a court of competent jurisdiction of having violated any provision of the federal fair housing laws, 42 U.S.C. Section 3601 et seq.;

18. Failure by a real estate broker, after the receipt of a commission, to render an accounting to and pay to a real estate licensee the licensee's earned share of the commission received;

19. Conviction in a court of competent jurisdiction in this or any other state of the crime of forgery, embezzlement, obtaining money under false pretenses, extortion, conspiracy to defraud, fraud, or any similar offense or offenses, or pleading guilty or nolo contendere to any such offense or offenses;

20. Advertising to buy, sell, rent, or exchange any real estate without disclosing that the licensee is a real estate licensee;

21. Paying any part of a fee, commission, or other valuable consideration received by a real estate licensee to any person not licensed;

22. Offering, loaning, paying, or making to appear to have been paid, a down payment or earnest money deposit for a purchaser or seller in connection with the real estate transaction;

23. Violation of the Residential Property Condition Disclosure Act.

Section 605:10-17-4 list the following "prohibited dealings" which include untrustworthy, improper, fraudulent, or dishonest dealings and are also subject to disciplinary action:

1. The making of a brokerage service contract without a date of termination.

2. Purchasing of property by a licensee for himself or herself or another entity in which the licensee has an interest as defined in 605:10-15-1 (c), if such property is listed with the broker or the broker's firm, without first making full disclosure thereof and obtaining the approval of the owner, or the failure by the licensee to exert the licensee's best effort in order to later purchase or acquire the property for himself or another entity in which he has an interest as defined in 605:10-15-1 (c).

3. Repeated misrepresentations, even though not fraudulent, which occur as a result of the failure by the licensee to inform himself or herself of pertinent facts concerning property, as to which he or she is performing services.

4. Procuring the signature to a purchase offer or contract or to any lease or lease proposal which has no definite purchase price or lease rental, or no method of payment, termination date, possession date, or property description.

5. The payment of any fees or amounts due the Commission with a check that is dishonored upon presentation to the bank on which the check is drawn.

6. Lending a broker's license to an associate; permitting an associate to operate as a broker; or failure of a broker to properly supervise the activities of an associate. A broker permitting the use of the broker's license to enable an associate licensed with

the broker to, in fact, establish and conduct a brokerage business wherein the broker's only interest is the receipt of a fee for the use of the broker's sponsorship.

7. Failure to make known in writing to any purchaser any interest the licensee has in the property they are selling.

8. Failure of the licensee to inform the buyer and seller in writing at the time the offer is presented that the buyer and seller will be expected to pay certain closing costs, brokerage service costs, and approximate amount of said costs.

9. Failure, upon demand in writing, to respond to a complaint in writing, or to disclose any information within licensee's knowledge, or to produce any document, book or record in licensee's possession or under licensee's control that is real estate related and under the jurisdiction of the Real Estate Commission, for inspection to a member of the Commission staff or any other lawful representative of the Commission.

10. Failure to reduce an offer to writing, when a proposed purchaser requests such offer to be submitted.

11. Failure to submit all bona fide offers to an owner when such offers are received prior to the seller accepting an offer in writing.

12. Any conduct in a real estate transaction which demonstrates bad faith or incompetency.

13. Failure to act, in marketing the licensee's own property, with the same good faith as when acting in the capacity of a real estate licensee.

14. An associate who does not possess the license of a broker or branch office broker as defined in the rules, but is intentionally acting in the capacity of a broker or branch office broker.

15. Discouraging a party from obtaining an inspection on a property.

16. Allowing access to, or control of, real property without the owner's authorization.

17. Knowingly providing false or misleading information to the Commission during the course of an investigation.

18. Interfering with an investigation by means of persuading, intimidating or threatening any party or witness, or tampering with or withholding evidence relating to the investigation.

19. Knowingly cooperating with an unlicensed person or entity to perform licensed real estate activities as required by Title 59 O.S. Section 858-301.

20. Failing to disclose any known immediate family relationship to a party to the transaction for which the broker is providing brokerage services.

21. Failure by a broker to ensure all persons performing real estate licensed activities under the broker are properly licensed.

22. An associate shall not perform licensed activities outside their broker's supervision.

23. Failing to maintain documents relating to a trust account or real estate transaction for the time period as required by Rule 605:10-13-1.

605:10-17-5 defines acts that are of a *substantial misrepresentation* nature and also subject to disciplinary actions:

(1) The recommendation or use by a licensee of a fictitious or false instrument for the purpose of inducing any lender or Government Agency to loan or insure any sum of money.

(2) Failure to disclose to a buyer or other cooperative licensee or firm a known material defect regarding the condition of a parcel of real estate of which a broker or associate has knowledge.

(3) The use by a real estate broker of the name or trade name of a licensee whose license has been revoked or currently on suspension.

(4) Representing to any lender, guaranteeing agency or any other interested party, either verbally or through the preparation of false documents, an amount in excess of the true and actual sales price of the real property or terms differing from those actually agreed upon by the parties to the transaction.

If the Commission determines the appropriate sanction is to suspend or revoke the license, they have the authority to do so. A person with a suspended or revoked license may not operate, directly or indirectly, or have a participating interest in a real estate brokerage entity. This also applies to an individual whose license is cancelled, surrendered, or lapsed pending investigation or disciplinary proceedings.

A licensee whose license has been suspended or revoked must return the license certificate and pocket identification card to the Commission office on or before the date the suspension or revocation becomes effective. When the suspension or revocation becomes effective the following requirements are imposed on the licensee:

1. The licensee shall not engage in any activity which requires a real estate license

2. When a broker's license is suspended/revoked, associates under the broker's supervision will automatically be placed "inactive" for the duration of the suspension/revocation period unless the licensee requests to be transferred to another broker.

3. If the suspended/revoked broker has a branch office, the license for the branch office will be placed inactive unless otherwise ordered by the Commission; and all licensees associated with the branch office will automatically be placed "inactive" for the duration of the suspension/revocation period unless the licensee requests to be transferred to another broker.

4. If a managing corporate broker of a corporation is suspended/revoked for an act which was on behalf of the corporation, the broker license of the corporation will be placed inactive unless otherwise ordered by the Commission; and all licensees associated with the corporation will automatically be placed "inactive" for the duration of the suspension/revocation period unless the licensee requests to be transferred to another broker.

5. If the managing partner(s) of a partnership is suspended/revoked for an act which was in behalf of the partnership, the broker license of the partnership will be placed inactive unless otherwise ordered by the Commission; and all licensees associated with the partnership will automatically be placed on "inactive" for the duration of the suspension/revocation period and the other broker will be placed "inactive" unless he or she requests his or her license to be transferred out of the partnership.

6. If a managing broker member of an association is suspended/revoked for an act which was in behalf of the association, the broker license of the association will be placed inactive unless otherwise ordered by the Commission; and all licensees associated with the association will automatically be placed "inactive" for the duration of the suspension/revocation period unless the licensee requests to be transferred to another broker.

7. A suspended/revoked licensee shall only receive compensation during the suspension/revocation period for acts which were performed during the period in which the licensee was actively licensed.

8. Listings must be cancelled by a suspended/revoked broker between the time the Order of suspension/revocation is received and the effective date of suspension/revocation, as listings will be void on the date the suspension/revocation becomes effective.

9. A suspended/revoked broker shall not assign listings to another broker without the written consent of the owner of the listed property.

10. A suspended/revoked broker shall not advertise real estate in any manner, and must remove and discontinue all advertising.

11. The telephone in a suspended/revoked broker's office shall not be answered in any manner to indicate the suspended/revoked broker is currently active in real estate.

12. All pending contracts, items or monies placed with the suspended/revoked broker must be transferred to another responsible broker as approved by the Commission and in compliance with Section 605:10-13-1 (n.).

13. A suspended/revoked licensee shall be required to comply with Section 605:10-13-1 (n) and provide the required information to the Commission prior to the effective date of suspension/revocation.

14. A representative of the Commission shall visit the office of any suspended/revoked broker prior to the effective date of the suspension/revocation to insure compliance with the requirements of (1) through (13) of this subsection.

A revoked, suspended, cancelled, surrendered or lapsed licensee is prohibited from performing licensed activities upon the effective date of loss of license.

Penalties against unlicensed persons – Any person unlicensed pursuant to the Oklahoma Real Estate License Code who willingly and knowingly violates any provision of the Code, upon conviction, shall be guilty of a misdemeanor punishable by a fine up to one thousand dollars ($1,000.00), or imprisonment in the county jail up to six (6) months, or both. In addition, the Oklahoma Real Estate Commission may impose a fine of up to five thousand dollars ($5,000.00) or the amount of the commission earned, whichever is greater for each violation; make application to the appropriate court for an order enjoining such acts or practices; issue an injunction or restraining order.

Penalties against licensees – The Oklahoma Real Estate Commission may impose administrative fines on any licensee licensed pursuant to the Oklahoma Real Estate License Code as follows:

- an administrative fine not less than one hundred dollars ($100.00) and no more than two thousand dollars ($2,000.00) for each violation; or
- up to five thousand dollars ($5,000.00) for multiple violations resulting from a single incident or transaction.

All administrative fines are due within thirty (30) days of notification and the license may be suspended until the fine is paid. If fines are not paid in full by the licensee within these 30 days, the fines double and the licensee has another 30-day period. If still not paid, the license will be automatically revoked.

Appeals – 605:10-1-3 addresses the appeal process for a licensee against whom a disciplinary action was taken. Any adverse administrative action or decision may be appealed by the adversely affected party filing within 30 days of notice of such action or decision through a written request for a hearing. The Secretary-Treasurer shall schedule an administrative decision hearing before a hearing examiner, a selected panel of the Commission, or the Commission as a whole, with at least 15 days' notice. The appealing party may present his or her own evidence or may present such through his or her counsel.

The rule goes into specific detail about the process involved with the hearing.

All parties will be furnished copies of the recommended order and notified as to the date the recommendations will be considered by the Commission for adoption. At the same time, notice will be given also to the parties that written exceptions or requests to present oral exceptions or arguments, if any, should be submitted on or before a designated date.

COMPLAINTS AND THE HEARING PROCESS

Any member of the public, including the Commission, may file a complaint against a licensee in writing on a form for such supplied by the Commission. The licensee is immediately notified and has fifteen (15) days to file an adequate written response. After the fifteen (15) day answer period, a field investigation or preliminary investigative session may be conducted to ascertain whether or not charges should be lodged and a formal hearing ordered. The secretary-treasurer of the Commission may designate an attorney who will act as prosecutor

OKLAHOMA REAL ESTATE COMMISSION COMPLAINT FORM
(Please Print in Black Ink or Use Typewriter)

Complaint Against:
_____
(Name)
_____
(Address)
_____
(City)   (State)   (Zip)
_____
(Telephone Number)

Chronological Statement of Complaint Facts:
_____
_____
_____
_____
_____

to examine the results of the field investigation and/or conduct a preliminary investigative session. The prosecutor may subpoena witnesses, take testimony by deposition, and compel the production of records and documents bearing upon the complaint. At the completion of the investigation, a written report of the findings shall be submitted to the Commission who shall then determine whether or not a formal hearing is required.

If the Commission finds that public health, safety, or welfare imperatively requires emergency action, a summary suspension may be ordered pending proceedings for revocation or other action within thirty (30) days.

In the event a formal hearing is sought, the Commission must give the licensee at least fifteen (15) days written notice, specifying the offenses of which the licensee is charged. If the licensee is an associate associated with a broker, the Commission will notify the broker as well. The hearing on such charges shall be set at such time and place as the Commission may prescribe. Each formal disciplinary hearing will be held before a hearing examiner, a selected panel of the Commission, or the Commission as a whole. All hearings are open to the public except that witnesses may be excluded from the hearing room when such witness is not testifying. A court reporter shall be present to record the proceedings.

Should the Commission determine that the licensee is guilty of a violation of the Code, such person may be disciplined in the manner as prescribed in the Code.

MISCELLANEOUS ISSUES §858-513 – §858-515.2

Psychologically impacted properties – The Code states that the fact or suspicion that real estate might be or is psychologically impacted, including:

- that an occupant of the real estate is, or was at any time suspected to be infected, or has been infected with Human Immunodeficiency Virus or diagnosed with Acquired Immune Deficiency Syndrome, or other disease which has been determined by medical evidence to be highly unlikely to be transmitted through the occupancy of a dwelling place; or
- that the real estate was, or was at any time suspected to have been the site of a suicide, homicide or other felony,

is *not* a material fact that must be disclosed in a real estate transaction. Remember from an earlier chapter, that licensees must disclose material facts about a property regardless of the party represented in the transaction. Oklahoma law here says that these matters pertaining to psychologically impacted properties are not required to be disclosed as they are not material facts.

Even though this information is not a material fact, in the event that a purchaser/lessee advises the licensee assisting the owner, in writing, that knowledge of these factors is important to the decision to purchase/lease the property, the licensee shall make inquiry of the owner and report any findings.

Registered sex offenders or violent crime offenders – Oklahoma regulation §858-514 states that despite the provisions of the Sex Offenders Registration Act and the Mary Rippy Violent Crime Offenders Registration Act, there is no duty upon a licensee to disclose any information regarding an offender required to register under such provisions.

Size of property §858-515.1 – The size or square footage of a subject property is not required to be provided by a licensee, and if it is provided, it is not considered any warranty or guarantee of the size.

Further, if the licensee provides any third-party information, such as from an appraisal, surveyor's or builder's plan, or tax records, the licensee must identify the source of the information. The Code goes into further detail regarding this matter.

Dual contracts – Dual contracts, either written or oral, are two contracts concerning the same parcel of real property, one of which states the true and actual purchase price and one of which states a purchase price in excess of the true and actual purchase price and is used as an inducement for mortgage investors to make a loan commitment on such real property in reliance upon the stated inflated value.

EDUCATION AND RECOVERY FUND

Most all states have created similar funds under similar names. The 600s address the fund in Oklahoma which has been created to serve two needs:

1. To serve as a source of funds for consumers who are injured financially as a result of the actions of a licensee; and
2. To provide educational programs for the further development of Oklahoma real estate licensees.

The fund is under the direct control and supervision of the Commission.

Monies in the fund shall be used to reimburse any claimant who has been awarded a judgment by a court of competent jurisdiction to have suffered monetary damages by an Oklahoma real estate licensee in any transaction, for which a license is required, of an act constituting a violation of the Oklahoma Real Estate License Code. The Commission may conduct an independent review of the case and may conduct a hearing to determine if a claim is eligible for recovery from the fund and the amount of damages that should be awarded.

Licensees contribute to the fund with each initial license application and subsequent renewal.

As in other states with such a fund, there is a defined process in the regulations that the consumer must follow to receive payment from the Education and Recovery Fund. In essence:

1. An action must be filed in district court based upon a violation specified in the Oklahoma Real Estate License Code;
2. The cause of action accrued not more than two (2) years prior to the filing of the action;
3. At the commencement of an action, the party filing the action shall immediately notify the Commission to this effect in writing and provide the Commission with a file-stamped copy of the petition or affidavit. Said Commission shall have the right to enter an appearance, intervene in, defend, or take any action it may deem appropriate to protect the integrity of the Fund. The Commission may waive the notification requirement if it determines that the public interest is best served by the waiver, that is to best meet the ends of justice and that the claimant making application made a good faith effort to comply with the notification requirements;
4. Final judgment is received by the claimant upon such action;
5. The final judgment is enforced as provided by statute for enforcement of judgments in other civil actions and that the amount realized was insufficient to satisfy the judgment; and
6. Any compensation recovered by the claimant from the judgment debtor, or from any other source for any monetary loss arising out of the cause of action, has been applied to the judgment awarded by the court.

A claim cannot be made against the fund if:

- The claimant is the spouse of the judgment debtor or a personal representative of such spouse;
- The claimant is a licensee who acted in their own behalf in the transaction which is the subject of the claim; or
- The claimant's claim is based upon a real estate transaction in which the claimant is, through their own action, jointly responsible for any resulting monetary loss with respect to the property owned or controlled by the claimant.

Should the claimant meet all of these conditions, the claimant may apply to the Commission for payment from fund equal to the unsatisfied portion of the judgment or $25,000, whichever is less. The claimant is entitled to reimbursement for attorney fees reasonably incurred in the litigation not to exceed twenty-five percent (25%) of the claimant's amount approved by the Commission.

Once a payment is made from the fund, the claimant assigns the claimant's right, title and interest in that portion of the judgment to the Commission which shall be subrogated up to the amount actually paid by the fund. Any amount subsequently recovered on the judgment by the Commission, to the extent of the Commission's right, title and interest therein, shall be used to reimburse the Oklahoma Real Estate Education and Recovery Fund.

Payments for claims are limited in the aggregate of $50,000 irrespective of the number of claimants or parcels of real estate involved in the transaction.

The second component of the fund is for education of Oklahoma's real estate licensees. The Code states that should the balance in the fund exceed $250,000, the Commission has the authority to expend funds for educational purposes:

- To promote the advancement of education in the field of real estate for the benefit of the general public and those licensed under the Oklahoma Real Estate License Code, but such promotion shall not be construed to allow advertising of this profession;
- To underwrite educational seminars and other forms of educational projects for the benefit of real estate licensees;
- To establish real estate courses at institutions of higher learning located in the state and accredited by the State Regents for Higher Education for the purpose of making such courses available to licensees and the general public; and
- To contract for a particular educational project in the field of real estate to further the purposes of the Oklahoma Real Estate License Code.

CHAPTER 1:
Laws and Rules Affecting Oklahoma Real Estate Practice
End of Chapter Quiz

1. Which of the following is FALSE regarding the Commission?

    a. The Commission consists of seven members.
    b. The commissioners must all have been Oklahoma residents the prior three years prior to appointment.
    c. All members must be real estate *brokers* with at least five years of active, full-time, experience.
    d. One member must be a lay person with no real estate experience.

2. Generally speaking, the services of real estate which require licensure include all of the following EXCEPT:

    a. sell
    b. advertise
    c. buy
    d. manage

3. Which of the following persons is NOT exempt from Oklahoma licensing?

    a. Smith is a one-fifth owner of Freeman Development, Inc. and handles all real estate transactions pertaining to properties Freeman Development, Inc. owns or acquires.
    b. Finnegan holds open houses and writes offers with purchasers on behalf of his real estate licensee friend, Thomas.
    c. Terry is an attorney-in-fact for his sister, Cathy, and is signing closing documents for real estate she owns.
    d. Dresen is an attorney-at-law and is reviewing the sales contract for his client Bernard in handling Bernard's bankruptcy.

4. Requirements for an Oklahoma real estate license include:

    a. providing a criminal history record
    b. 21 years of age or older
    c. successful completion of a 60 clock hour course of study approved by the Commission.
    d. all of these

5. The Oklahoma *provisional license* is valid for a period of:

    a. six months.
    b. 12 months.
    c. two years.
    d. three years.

6. Prior to the expiration of the provisional license, a salesperson must successfully complete what number of approved course hours representing *post-license education* real estate instruction?

    a. 30
    b. 45
    c. 60
    d. 90

7. A non-resident of Oklahoma may obtain an Oklahoma non-resident license by:

    a. successfully completing the Oklahoma state portion of the real estate examination.
    b. appointing the secretary-treasurer of the Commission as service agent.
    c. giving written consent that law suits may be commenced against the licensee in any county in the state where any cause of action may arise.
    d. all of these

8. An applicant who wishes to reapply for licensure after having her license revoked may not reapply until at least:

    a. one year of the Commission's determination of guilt.
    b. three years after the effective date of the revocation.
    c. five years from the conclusion of the formal hearing.
    d. ten years of the date of revocation.

9. Pertaining to the state exam:

    a. candidates who do not pass the exam may retake subsequent exams upon the payment of the required fees.
    b. a passing score of 75% is required.
    c. passing results are good for one year.
    d. all of these

10. Which of these is TRUE regarding Oklahoma real estate licenses?

    a. The term of the provisional salesperson license is two years.
    b. The term for all other licenses than the provisional license is two years.
    c. Licenses expire on the licensee's birthday in the month of expiration.
    d. none of these

11. The continuing education requirement to renew a salesperson's license (not the provisional license) is a minimum of:

    a. 21 hours.
    b. 24 hours.
    c. 30 hours.
    d. 45 hours.

12. Which of the following statements is TRUE?

    a. A name change of a licensee must be filed with the Commission within 10 days of occurrence.
    b. Any change of business address or office telephone number of a broker must be filed in the Commission office within 10 days.
    c. Associates must notify the Commission within 10 days of a change in home address.
    d. all of these

13. Regarding advertising restrictions upon a licensee:

    a. Yard signs must include the name of the real estate firm but need not include the broker's office telephone number.
    b. Advertising may be somewhat misleading but may not be fraudulent or discriminatory in any way.
    c. A broker is not required to secure the permission of the owner to advertise a property.
    d. none of these

14. Which of these actions could cause a licensee to be disciplined by the Commission?

    a. Advertising to buy, sell, rent, or exchange any real estate without disclosing that the licensee is a real estate licensee.
    b. Paying any part of a commission, or other valuable consideration, received by a real estate licensee to any person not licensed.
    c. Failure to make known in writing to any purchaser any interest the licensee has in the property the licensee is selling.
    d. all of these

15. Violations of the licensing law include:

    a. suspension of license.
    b. revocation of license.
    c. a fine up to $2,000 for each violation.
    d. all of these

16. If the Commission finds that the public health, safety, or welfare imperatively requires emergency action to prevent a licensee from practicing, the Commission may serve upon the licensee a(n):

    a. summary suspension.
    b. cease and desist order.
    c. injunction.
    d. stop order.

17. Which of these is considered a *material fact* per Oklahoma licensing law and therefore required to be disclosed?

    a. The occupant of the home being sold is infected with AIDS.
    b. The roof has two separate leaks.
    c. The home was the site of a suicide.
    d. A registered sex offender lives next door.

18. A claim against the Education and Recovery Fund may be successful if:

    a. The claimant is the spouse of the licensee.
    b. The claimant is a licensee who acted in his own behalf in the transaction.
    c. The claimant files the action within two years of the offense.
    d. The claimant, is through his own action, jointly responsible for any resulting monetary loss.

19. Regarding payment from the *Education and Recovery Fund*:

    a. Payment will be equal to the unsatisfied portion of the judgment up to $25,000.
    b. The claimant is entitled to reimbursement for attorney fees up to 25% of the claimant's approved amount.
    c. Payments are limited in the aggregate of $50,000 irrespective of the number of claimants or parcels involved.
    d. all of these

20. Oklahoma requirements for licensure as a broker include:

    a. three years' experience within the previous five years as a licensee.
    b. completion of the *Advanced Course in Real Estate*.
    c. successful completion of 60 clock hours of advanced real estate instruction.
    d. all of these

Chapter 2

Oklahoma Broker
Relationships Act

The Oklahoma Real Estate Commission amended the Oklahoma Broker Relationships Act effective November 1, 2013. If a consumer believes a licensee has failed to comply with this Act, that consumer is encouraged to contact the Oklahoma Real Estate Commission.

BROKER'S DUTIES TO *ALL* PARTIES IN A TRANSACTION

Every Oklahoma real estate broker, has the following duties to *all parties* in every real estate transaction conducted in the state. These duties are mandated by law (858-353) and may not be abrogated (struck or appealed) or waived by a broker. Because licensees affiliated with the broker are an "extension" of the broker, these duties "extend" to these affiliated licensees as well. The duties are:

1. Treat all parties with honesty and exercise reasonable skill and care;

2. Unless specifically waived in writing by a party to the transaction:

   a. receive all written offers and counteroffers,
   b. reduce offers or counteroffers to a written form upon request of any party to a transaction, and
   c. present timely all written offers and counteroffers;

3. Timely account for all money and property received by the broker;

4. Keep confidential information received from a party or prospective party confidential.

The confidential information shall not be disclosed by a firm without the consent of the party disclosing the information, unless:

- consent to the disclosure is granted, in writing, by the party or prospective party disclosing the information,
- the disclosure is required by law, or
- the information is made public, or becomes public, as the result of actions from a source other than the firm.

The following information shall be considered "confidential" and shall be the only information considered "confidential" in a transaction:

- that a party or prospective party is **willing to pay more** or **accept less** than what is being offered;

- that a party or prospective party is willing to agree to *financing terms* that are different from those offered;
- the *motivating factors* of the party or prospective party purchasing, selling, leasing, optioning, or exchanging the property; and
- information *specifically designated as confidential* by a party unless such information is public.

5. Disclose information pertaining to the property as required by the *Residential Property Condition Disclosure Act*; and

6. Comply with all requirements of The Oklahoma Real Estate License Code and all applicable statutes and rules.

BROKER'S ADDITIONAL DUTIES TO A PARTY *RECEIVING THE BROKER'S SERVICES*

In addition to the duties above, which every Oklahoma real estate broker has to *all* parties in every real estate transaction conducted in the state, a broker has the following duties and responsibilities *only to* a party for whom the broker is *providing brokerage services*. Again, these are mandatory and may not be abrogated or waived.

- inform the party, in writing, when an offer is made, that the party will be expected to pay certain costs, brokerage service costs, and approximate amount of costs; and
- keep the party informed regarding the transaction

When working with both parties to a transaction, these duties and responsibilities shall be owed to both parties.

BROKERAGE AGREEMENTS

Section 858-355.1 addresses requirements of the verbiage to be contained within the brokerage agreements between Oklahoma brokers and the parties for whom they provide services.

The section starts with the requirement that all brokerage agreements shall incorporate the duties and responsibilities as described previously to all parties in a transaction and to parties for whom the broker is providing brokerage services. The law goes on to say that a broker may provide brokerage services either to one, or to both parties in a transaction, but whomever the broker is providing services to, must receive a written disclosure and description of those duties and responsibilities. Additionally, that disclosure must be made *prior to the party signing a contract* (to sell, purchase, lease, option, or exchange).

Should an Oklahoma real estate firm elect to provide brokerage services to *both parties* in a transaction, the firm must provide written notice to both parties that the firm is providing brokerage services to both parties. This is referred to as **informed consent** in the national portion of this course. Further, this disclosure, too, must be made prior to the both parties signing a contract.

Section 858-355.1 also states that should a broker intend to provide fewer brokerage services than those normally required to complete a transaction, the broker must disclose, in writing, a description of those steps in the transaction for which the broker will not provide brokerage services, and also state that the broker assisting the other party in the transaction, is not required to provide assistance with these steps in any manner.

858-356 Confirmation – Not only must the broker disclose the duties and responsibilities as described in the opening of this chapter, in writing, prior to the party or parties entering a contract, but those duties and responsibilities must then be **confirmed**, or stated again, in a separate paragraph in the contract, at time of contract, or on an attachment to the contract. The Oklahoma Real Estate Commission provides Oklahoma brokers an *Oklahoma Uniform Contract of Sale of Real Estate* for residential sales. Along with the six-page contract, the Commission has also provided an Acknowledgement and Confirmation of Disclosures whereby the parties confirm they have received the disclosure of the brokerage services in writing along with other relative disclosures such as the Residential Property Condition Disclosure or Disclaimer Form and others. The contract and the confirmation of disclosures can be found at the back of chapter 12.

You can probably sense the seriousness of the Oklahoma Commission and Legislature as to this disclosure. If you think they might be going a little overboard, this is very common in most all states.

TERMINATION OF RELATIONSHIP

Oklahoma law states there are no duties owed by the broker to a party for whom services were provided after the termination of the relationship, whether the relationship ended by termination (one parties "fires" the other), expiration, or performance of all duties. There are, however, two exceptions. The broker must:

- account for all monies and property relating to the transaction; and
- keep confidential all confidential information received by the broker during the broker's relationship with the party.

Compensation – Consistent with the national portion of this course, and as seen in many other states, the issue of compensation has little or nothing to do with establishing a relationship, terminating a relationship, or breaching a relationship, between a broker and a party to a real estate transaction in Oklahoma. This is codified in section 858-359.

2013 AMENDMENT

Section 858-360 establish a very important point: everything adopted in the 2013 amendment (and summarized in this chapter thus far), which is codified as 858-351 through 858-363, ***replaces and abrogates*** fiduciary duties and other duties as established in common law principles of agency. This means, if you read something in the agency chapter in the national portion of this course that contradicts with content within this chapter, the material in *this* chapter overrides and supersedes as it pertains to real estate practice in Oklahoma.

Notice some fairly normal vocabulary has been *removed* from this chapter. Oklahoma no longer uses verbiage such as:

- ~~agency~~
- ~~sub-agency~~
- ~~fiduciary duties~~
- ~~dual agent~~

- ~~represent~~
- ~~client~~
- ~~customer~~

Notice, instead, the new law uses terminology such as "party to whom the broker is providing brokerage services" instead of "client," and "can provide brokerage services to both parties in a transaction" rather than "dual agent." Oklahoma uses the word "relationships" instead of "agency." These are some rather significant, perhaps even, radical, changes.

This author suggests the student not allow the differences between Oklahoma broker relationships law and national "agency" terminology as seen elsewhere in this course, confuse, worry, or frustrate you. It is prudent to be aware of the technical distinctions even in practice. You will be working with buyers, sellers, and licensees from other parts of the country who are going to be accustomed to the practices as described in the national portion of the course and your job will be to inform them of Oklahoma procedures.

Vicarious Liability – Also in the national portion of this course, you may have discovered ***vicarious liability***. This concept holds a client liable for the wrongful acts or omissions of the real estate licensee acting on his behalf. Besides removing terms like "client," section 858-362 adds a "party" to a transaction shall not be subject to vicarious liability.

Associates of real estate broker – Each broker associate, sales associate, and provisional sales associate shall be associated with a real estate broker. A real estate broker may authorize associates to enter into written agreements to provide brokerage services in the name of the real estate broker.

CHAPTER 2:
Oklahoma Broker Relationships Act
End of Chapter Quiz

1. An Oklahoma broker may enter into a written brokerage agreement to provide real estate services as a:

   a. single-party broker.
   b. transaction broker.
   c. dual agent.
   d. none of these

2. Which of these is a duty to only to a party for whom the broker is providing brokerage services as opposed to all parties in a transaction?

   a. exercise reasonable skill and care
   b. present all written offers and counteroffers in a timely manner
   c. inform the party when an offer is made of approximate amount of costs
   d. keep confidential information confidential

3. Which of the following is *not* considered confidential information?

   a. That a party is willing to pay more or accept less than what is being offered.
   b. That a party is willing to agree to financing terms that are different from those offered.
   c. The original price the seller paid for the property.
   d. The motivating factors of the party purchasing or selling.

4. Which of the following statements is FALSE?

   a. The broker must disclose his duties in writing before the party enters a contract.
   b. The broker must disclose his duties in writing again at the time his party enters a contract.
   c. If the broker chooses to offers less services than are required to complete a transaction, he may do so without further obligation.
   d. An Oklahoma broker may not be an agent, sub-agent, or dual agent.

5. Which of the following statements is INCORRECT?

   a. The broker must only represent the party who pays the broker's commission.
   b. A party to a real estate transaction shall *not* be vicariously liable for the acts or omissions of a real estate licensee.
   c. A real estate broker may authorize associates to enter into written agreements to provide services in the name of the broker.
   d. Oklahoma real estate licensees do *not* have fiduciary duties.

Chapter 3

Property Management and the Nonresidential/Residential Landlord and Tenant Acts

This chapter shall address a broad overview of property management and specifically covers Oklahoma's Nonresidential/Residential Landlord and Tenant Acts.

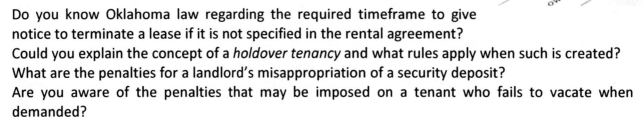

DO YOU KNOW???

Do you know Oklahoma law regarding the required timeframe to give notice to terminate a lease if it is not specified in the rental agreement?

Could you explain the concept of a *holdover tenancy* and what rules apply when such is created?

What are the penalties for a landlord's misappropriation of a security deposit?

Are you aware of the penalties that may be imposed on a tenant who fails to vacate when demanded?

What happens to a leasehold when there is a change of ownership to the property?

These are just some of the topics to be covered in this chapter.

OVERVIEW OF PROPERTY MANAGEMENT

Much of this textbook zeroed in on the relationship of real estate licensees with either sellers or buyers. Property management is another form of an agency relationship where the property owner is the principal and the property manager is the agent of the property owner. In the chapter entitled *Agency and the Practice of Real Estate* in the national portion, a general orientation was provided explaining the goals and practices of property managers with respect to fulfilling their duties to the owners who employ them.

Real estate property managers are hired to oversee residential, commercial, or industrial properties for owners who are unable or unwilling to handle the details of renting, collecting rents, property maintenance and repair, and record keeping associated with property ownership. Property managers are charged with the dual goal of maximizing the rental income from the property while at the same time preserving the property's worth. In fulfilling responsibilities to the owner, however, the property manager is also charged with safeguarding the civil rights, health, and safety of the tenants.

Property management activities include showing real property for rent or lease; soliciting tenants and landlords; negotiating on behalf of the tenant or landlord; and compliance with the **Oklahoma Non-Residential and Residential Landlord and Tenant Acts**. Performance of these services for compensation requires an active real estate license.

Property managers manage residential properties from single family homes to multi-unit apartment buildings as well as office buildings and shopping centers on the commercial side. In addition to securing tenants, a property manager handles bookkeeping and reporting on behalf of the owner. The agent must comply with laws pertaining to leases, fair housing, agency, and landlord-tenant relationships.

Kindly review the property management agreement used by the Greater Tulsa Association of REALTORS® on the following pages to become better acquainted with the requirements of such an agreement, including:

- the names of the parties clearly identified
- the duties and responsibilities of the manager as well as the manager's scope of authority
- an accurate property description
- reporting requirements
- brokerage fee
- the handling of funds and payments to third parties
- the handling of security deposits and prepaid rents
- the effective date and termination date
- conditions for termination of the agreement
- signatures of the parties

RESIDENTIAL PROPERTY MANAGEMENT &
EXCLUSIVE RIGHT TO LEASE AGREEMENT

THIS AGREEMENT is entered into by and between _____(Owner) and_____(Broker)_____ day of _____ and upon approval by both Owner and Broker as evidenced by their signatures hereto, a valid and binding Property Management and Leasing Agreement shall exist, the terms and conditions of which are as follows:

1. **Appointment of Broker and Legal Description of Property.** The Owner engages and appoints the Broker as the sole and exclusive Manager and Rental Broker of the following:

> **Street Address:** _____

> **Legal Description:** _____(the "Property").

2. **Term.** This Agreement incorporates both the Exclusive Right to Lease the Property and the Agreement to Manage the Property and the term for each shall be:

> **a. The term of this Exclusive Right to Lease Listing Agreement** begins on _____, and expires (except for the provisions of paragraph ( ) at midnight on _____, .

> **b. The term of this Property Management Agreement** shall begin upon the execution of a lease and occupancy of the Property by a tenant and shall remain in force for a period of _____

> _____ and year-to-year thereafter.

> **c. Owner understands and agrees that the Broker will not provide the care, maintenance and management of the Property until the deposits provided for in Paragraph 8 are received.**

3. **Authorization.** The Owner confers on the Broker the sole power and authority to negotiate as Broker for the Owner. Broker is authorized to negotiate, prepare, and execute all leases, including all renewals and extensions of leases and to cancel and modify existing leases. All cost of leasing shall be paid by the Owner.

4. **Broker Relationships.** Broker's relationship with Owner and duties under that relationship as provided under the *Broker Relationship Act* are set in paragraph 29 of this Agreement. At the time of any initial contact, Broker shall inform all prospective tenants and their brokers, of the relationship Broker has with Owner. The Broker also agrees to use Broker's best efforts to lease and keep leased and occupied all space in the Property, and to collect and to receive all rents and other income due and payable from tenants.

5. **Compensation.** The Owner agrees that:
    a. On the commencement of the term of the Property Management Agreement and anytime during the Property Management Agreement, the Property is vacant, Broker shall be paid a vacancy fee of _____ per month until the Property is leased.
    b. The Broker shall be paid a leasing fee of _____ of the first full month's rental or _____, whichever is greater and lease renewal fee of _____.
    c. The Broker shall be paid a management fee of _____of each month's rental during the term of the lease and any renewals of said lease.
    d. If Tenant or prospective Tenant purchases the Property or the Property is purchased for the benefit of and/or on behalf of the tenant during the term of this Agreement or within _____ days of the expiration of the Listing Agreement or the Property Management Agreement, whichever expires last, Owner agrees to pay the undersigned Broker a sales commission of _____ of the sales price.

If during the term of this Agreement, the Owner shall offer the Property for sale or exchange, the Broker shall have the exclusive right to offer the Property for sale or exchange under such terms and conditions as agreed to in writing by the Owner and Broker.

6. **Marketing of Property.** During the term of this Agreement Owner authorizes Broker to advertise the lease of the Property by classified advertising and/or Web site advertising. Owner agrees to pay the actual cost of any classified advertising.

Residential Property Management & Exclusive Right to Lease Agreement (Continued)

7. Security Deposits. Broker shall collect, deposit, and disburse tenant's security deposits in an FDIC approved Trust Account in the State of Oklahoma in accordance with the Landlord Tenant Act and the tenant's lease agreement. It is understood and agreed by all parties that these funds may be deposited into a FDIC insured interest bearing account with the Broker retaining the interest to compensate for the cost and burden of maintaining such an account. Any other interest paid on the operating accounts or the Trust Account will also be retained by the Broker.

8. Initial Deposits and Contingency Reserve. Immediately upon commencement of this Agreement, Owner shall remit to Broker the sum of $_____ to be deposited in the Operating and/or Reserve Accounts as an initial deposit representing the estimated disbursements to be made in the first month following the commencement of this Agreement, plus an additional sum of $_____ as a contingency reserve. Owner agrees to maintain the contingency reserve stated above at all times in the Operating and/or Reserve Account(s) to enable Broker to pay the obligations of Owner under this Agreement as they become due. Owner and Broker shall review the amount of the contingency reserve from time to time and shall agree in writing on a new contingency reserve amount when such is required.

9. Operating and/or Reserve Account(s). Broker shall establish a separate account known as_____ _____ Trust Account separate and apart from Broker's corporate accounts, for the deposit of receipts collected as described herein, in a bank or other institution whose deposits are insured by the federal government. Such depository shall be selected by the Broker. However, Broker shall not be held liable in the event of bankruptcy or failure of a depository. Funds in the Operating and/or Reserve Account(s) remain the property of the Owner subject to disbursement of expenses by the Broker as described in this Agreement.

10. Expenses of the Owner. All operating and maintenance expenses, including expense of advertising and annual audit, shall constitute deductions from gross annual rentals in addition to the fee specified in paragraph 5. Where Broker is acting as Owner's General Contractor for purposes other than ordinary maintenance due to ordinary wear and tear, the Broker shall be paid a supervision fee of _____.

11. Deductions from Rental Income. Owner agrees the Broker shall be entitled to deduct from the monthly rental income any earned commissions, fees, or other obligations the Owner has authorized the Broker to pay on behalf of the Owner. If the Broker is authorized to pay the Owner's monthly mortgage payments, including taxes and insurance, or any other expense assessed on the Property, the Owner must maintain enough money in the Owner's account deposited in _____ Owner's Trust Account to allow for such payment plus any other fees required to maintain the Owner's Property. In the event any rent check previously collected and accounted for is returned insufficient an

appropriate adjustment in the fee and balance paid to Owner shall be made in the next ensuing month. Payment of the first mortgage is a service and shall not be construed as a liability on the part of the Broker.

12. Special Charges. If permitted by applicable law, Broker may collect and retain from tenants any or all of the following: an administrative charge for late payment of rent, a charge for returned or non-negotiable checks, a credit report fee, and administrative charge and Broker's commission for sub-leasing. Broker need not account to Owner for such charges or Broker's commission for sub-leasing.

13. Payment of Expenses. The Owner authorizes the Broker to pay all expenses as hereinafter provided to the extent funds are available from rental income or funds from the Owner for the operating, maintenance, and repair of the Property and equipment. In the event funds from rental income or funds from Owner shall fail to pay any such bills and assessments when due, Owner shall be liable for any assessments, legal fees, court costs, interest or any other penalties that are incurred as a result of such failure to pay the bill.

14. Disbursement of Net Proceeds. Each month, Broker will remit any net proceeds, in excess of that amount deemed necessary by Broker to meet operational expenses and provide a detailed statement of receipts, disbursements and charges. Such remittance, shall be made payable to Owner and mailed to address listed below or deposited electronically via separate authorization. In the event disbursements are in excess of rents collected, Owner agrees to pay such excess promptly upon demand and understands that Broker may terminate this agreement if the excess is not paid.

15. Maintenance of Property. The Owner authorizes the Broker to manage and maintain, at Owner's expense, the Property and Owner's equipment therein. Owner agrees that Broker shall only use the services of independent contractors

Residential Property Management & Exclusive Right to Lease Agreement (Continued)

who carry and are covered by liability and workmen's compensation insurance (or have a workman's compensation insurance waiver).

16. Maintenance of Records. The Broker agrees to keep and maintain at all times all necessary books and records relating to the leasing, management and operation of the unit.

17. Approval of Contracts. Before entering into any contract, the Broker agrees to obtain approval of the Owner for repairs, replacements, or any other maintenance expense which contracts involve an expenditure of more than $_____. In the event of an emergency however, for the protection of the Property and its tenants, the Broker shall have power to take the necessary action without obtaining the Owner's consent. The Broker will inform Owner of such emergency action taken as soon as practicable.

18. Enforcement of Leases. The Owner authorizes the Broker to make all reasonable efforts to enforce the terms of the lease, in accordance with the Oklahoma Residential Landlord Tenant Act and any applicable Fair Debt Collection Practices Act (FDCPA). Owner agrees to pay the costs, including legal fees, incurred by Broker for such enforcement.

19. Legal Fees for Legal Advice. Upon Owners authorization Broker may obtain legal assistance regarding issues affecting the Property. Owner shall also pay the expense of any legal advise or proceedings affecting the Property.

20. Owner Responsible For All Expenses of Litigation: Owner shall pay all expenses incurred by Broker, including, but not limited to, reasonable attorney's fees, Broker's costs, Broker's time, any liability, fines, penalties or the like, in connection with any claim, proceeding, or suit involving an alleged violation by Broker or Owner, or both, of any law pertaining to fair employment, fair credit reporting, environmental protection, rent control, taxes, or fair housing, including, but not limited to, any law prohibiting or making illegal discrimination on the basis of race, sex, creed, color, religion, national origin, mental or physical handicap, or familial status provided, however, that Owner shall not be responsible to Broker for any such expenses in the event Broker if finally adjudged to have personally, and not in representative capacity, violated any such law. Nothing contained in this Agreement shall obligate Broker to employ legal counsel to represent Owner in any such proceeding or suit.

21. Broker's Authorization. All persons contracted for, or to be contracted for the maintenance and repair of the Property, shall be under the control of the Broker. Notwithstanding this authority, it is recognized that such persons are the contractors of the Owner and not contractors of the Broker.

22. Owner's indemnification. The Owner shall indemnify and save harmless the Broker from and against all claims, losses and liabilities with respect to the Property and arising out of or related to the leasing and managing agency established by this Agreement (including costs and attorney's fees), saving and excepting only those resulting from, arising out of or occasioned by the gross negligence or willful misconduct of the Broker or its employees.

23. Broker Assumes No Liability. Broker assumes no liability whatsoever for any acts of omissions of Owner, or any previous Owners or Agents or Tenants of the Property. Broker assumes no liability for any failure of or default by any Tenant in the payment of any rent or other charges due Owner or in the performance of any obligations owed by a Tenant to Owner pursuant to any lease or otherwise. The Broker does not assume any liability for previously unknown violations of environmental or any other regulations, which may become known during the period this Agreement is in effect. Any such regulatory violations or hazards discovered by Broker will be brought to the attention of Owner in writing, and Owner shall promptly cure them with no liability for the Broker.

24. Insurance: On execution of this Agreement, Owner will review existing coverage with his insurance broker to determine adequacy of coverage and to change policy to a rental policy. Owner agrees to carry bodily injury, property damage and personal injury liability insurance in limits of not less than Three Hundred Thousand Dollars ($300,000). The Owner will not hold Broker liable for any Tenant damages or damages incurred by third party or any violations of law by Tenant. Owner agrees to name Broker as additional insured and to provide a copy of the policy for the file.

25. Furnishing Documents: Owner agrees to promptly furnish Broker all documents and records required to properly manage the Property, including, but not limited to leases (including amendments and pertinent correspondence relating thereto), status of rental payments, loan payment information, and copies of existing service contracts.

26. Termination: Owner or Broker may terminate this Agreement at any time with a _____ day written notice with notice and settlement by Owner of final expenses.

Residential Property Management and Leasing Agreement (Continued)

27. Fair Housing. As provided in Oklahoma's Landlord Tenant Regulations, Owner and/or Broker shall not deny or terminate tenancy to a blind, deaf or physically handicapped person because of the guide, signal or service dog of such person unless such dogs are specifically prohibited in the rental agreement entered into prior to November 1, 1985.

As provided by Federal law, Owner and Broker shall not refuse to lease or rent or refuse to negotiate for the lease or rent of the Property or otherwise make the Property unavailable to any person because of race, color, religion, sex, familial status or national origin.

28. Additional Fees. See attached addendum for additional fees, if any.

29. Broker Relationship. By entering into this written agreement, the REALTOR® shall provide services as a **Single-party Broker,** which shall be deemed to include, and which may not abrogate or waive, the mandatory duties and responsibilities set forth in this section:
1. To treat all parties with honesty and exercise reasonable skill and care;
2. To be available to:
   a. receive all written offers and counteroffers,
   b. reduce offers or counteroffers to a written form upon request of any party to a transaction
   c. present timely all written offers and counter offers.
3. To inform in writing the party for whom the Broker is providing services when an offer is made that the party will be expected to pay certain closing costs, [if applicable] brokerage service costs and approximate amount of said costs.
4. To keep the party for whom the Single-party Broker is performing services informed regarding the transaction.
5. To account timely for all money and property received by the Broker.
6. To keep confidential information received from a party confidential. Unless required by law, the Broker shall **not** without the express permission of the respective party, disclose the following confidential information to the other party:
   ♦ That a party is willing to pay more or accept less than what is being offered,
   ♦ That a party is willing to agree to rental terms that are different from those offered; and
   ♦ The motivation of either party in leasing, selling or purchasing the Property.
7. To perform all brokerage activities for the benefit of the party for whom the Single-party Broker is performing services unless prohibited by law.
8. To obey the specific directions of the party for whom the Single-party Broker is performing services that are not contrary to the terms of a contract between the parties to the transaction; and
9. To comply with all requirements of the Oklahoma Real Estate License Code and all applicable statutes and rules.

Specific Directions. The Landlord and Broker agree that the specific directions provided for in the *Broker Relationship Act* shall be in writing, and that Landlord shall pay any costs Broker incurs in complying with such instructions.

Vicarious Liability. The Landlord understands the Landlord may be vicariously liable for the actions and words of the Broker or Broker's affiliated real estate licensees providing services for the Landlord.

30. Property Condition.

a. FLOOD NOTIFICATION. Have you been notified by any City or County governmental agency, or are you aware that the Property is in a flood hazard area? ☐ yes ☐ no.

In order to fulfill Landlord's and Broker's obligations of disclosure, if the Property has been flooded within the past five (5) years and such fact is known to the Landlord, the Landlord shall disclose such information. As

provided in the Landlord Tenant Act, the landlord shall include such information prominently and in writing as part of any written rental agreements. Failure to provide such information entitles a Tenant who is a party to the rental agreement to sue the Landlord of the premises in a court of appropriate jurisdiction and to recover the personal property damages sustained by the Tenant from flooding of the premises.

b. LEAD-BASED PAINT DISCLOSURE. Lead-Based Paint Disclosure. If Property was built prior to 1978, Landlord shall complete the Disclosure and Acknowledgment of Lead-Based Paint and as provided under Federal

Residential Property Management and Leasing Agreement (Continued)

Statute a copy of the Disclosure along with a copy of the pamphlet *Protect Your Family from Lead in Your Home*, shall be provided to potential tenants.

c. OTHER PROPERTY DEFECTS. To fulfill Landlord's and Broker's obligations of disclosure, Landlord will disclose any Property defects he has knowledge of and Broker shall disclose such defects to a potential tenant.

31. GTAR. *Landlord and tenants You Need to Know!* Landlord received a copy of, read and understands the **GTAR** *Landlords and Tenants You Need to Know!* document, **which includes an explanation of Single-party and Transaction Broker Relationships.** The Landlord further understands and agrees that a copy shall also be provided to potential Tenants.

32. Notices: All notices to be given by either party to the other shall be given by personal delivery or certified mail and shall be effective on receipt. Notices to the respective parties shall be addressed as follows:

Landlord:
Mailing Address_____

Phone_____ Fax_____ E-Mail_____

Social Security Number_____

Insurance Company_____ Policy #_____

Insurance Agent_____ Phone #_____

Broker:

Mailing Address_____

Phone_____ Fax_____ E-Mail_____

In the event either party's address changes, 30-day written notice shall be given to the other party.

APPROVED AND AGREED TO BY OWNER

This _____ day of _____

_____

_____

APPROVED AND AGREED TO BY BROKER

This _____ day of _____

_____

_____

LANDLORD AND TENANT LAWS REGARDING NONRESIDENTIAL RENTAL PROPERTY

Oklahoma statutes define **nonresidential rental property** as any land or building which is rented or leased to a tenant for other than residential purposes and the rental agreement of which is not regulated under the provisions of the *Oklahoma Residential Landlord Tenant Act*.

Personal property – If a tenant abandons, surrenders possession of, or is evicted from nonresidential rental property, and leaves personal property on the premises, the landlord may take possession of the personal property ten (10) days after the tenant receives personal service of notice or fifteen (15) days after notice is mailed, whichever is latest. If the personal property has no apparent value, the landlord may dispose of the property. Or, the landlord may sell the personal property at a public sale. Payment by the tenant of all outstanding rent, damages, storage fees, court costs and attorneys' fees shall be a prerequisite to the return of the personal property.

The landlord is required to store personal property of the tenant in a place of safe-keeping either on the premises or to commercial storage, either of which can incur storage costs that must be paid by the tenant in order to regain possession. If the tenant fails to take possession of the personal property, the property shall be deemed abandoned and the landlord may then sell the property without liability to the tenant.

The landlord may not be held responsible for damages by reason of the landlord's election to destroy, sell, or otherwise dispose of the personal property in compliance with the act unless the landlord deliberately or negligently violated the provisions in which case the landlord is liable for actual damages.

Any proceeds from the sale or other disposition of the personal property shall be applied by the landlord in the following order:

1. To the reasonable expenses of taking, holding, preparing for sale or disposition, giving notice and selling or disposing thereof;
2. To the satisfaction of any properly recorded security interest;
3. To the satisfaction of any amount due from the tenant to the landlord for rent or otherwise; and
4. The balance, if any, shall be paid into court within thirty (30) days of the sale and held for six (6) months and, if not claimed by the owner of the personal property within that period, shall escheat to the county.

RESIDENTIAL LANDLORD AND TENANT ACT

This act applies to, regulates and determines rights, obligations and remedies under a rental agreement, for a dwelling unit located in Oklahoma.

Lack of agreement – The first order of business established within the act is to address common issues if the verbiage of the rental agreement either does not address, is unclear, or the parties do not agree as to the terms of that issue. As an example, the Act states that in the absence of agreement, the occupants of a dwelling unit shall pay to the landlord as rent the fair rental value for the use and occupancy of the dwelling unit. As another example, unless the rental agreement fixes a definite term in writing, the tenancy is week-to-week in the case of a roomer or boarder who pays weekly rent, and in all other cases month-to-month.

Termination – The Act addresses termination of an Oklahoma tenancy such that when the tenancy is month-to-month or tenancy at will, the landlord or tenant may terminate the tenancy provided the landlord or tenant gives a written notice to the other at least thirty (30) days before the date upon which the termination is to become effective. When the tenancy is less than month-to-month, the landlord or tenant may terminate the tenancy provided the landlord or tenant gives to the other a written notice served of at least seven (7) days before the date upon which the termination is to become effective. Unless otherwise agreed upon, a tenancy for a definite term expires on the ending date thereof without notice.

An **estate at sufferance** is created if the tenant remains in possession without the landlord's consent after the expiration of the term of the rental agreement, or its termination under the Oklahoma Residential Landlord and Tenant Act, the landlord may immediately bring an action for possession and damages. If the tenant's holdover is willful and not in good faith, the landlord may also recover an amount not more than twice the average monthly rental, computed and prorated on a daily basis, for each month or portion thereof that said tenant remains in possession. A **holdover tenancy** exists if the landlord consents to the tenant's continued occupancy, a month-to-month tenancy is thus created, unless the parties otherwise agree.

Notice to terminate – Notice to terminate any tenancy shall be served on the tenant or landlord personally unless otherwise specified by law. If the tenant cannot be located, service shall be made by delivering the notice to any family member of such tenant over the age of twelve (12) years residing with tenant. If service cannot be made on the tenant personally or on such family member, notice shall be posted at a conspicuous place on the dwelling unit of the tenant. If the notice is posted, a copy of such notice shall be mailed to the tenant by certified mail. If service cannot be made on the landlord personally, the notice shall be mailed to the landlord by certified mail.

Unenforceable provisions – §113 of the Act lists provisions that must *not* be created in a rental agreement including that either party:

1. agrees to waive or forego rights or remedies under this act;

2. authorizes any person to confess judgment on a claim arising out of the rental agreement;
3. agrees to pay the other party's attorney's fees;
4. agrees to the exculpation, limitation or indemnification of any liability arising under law for damages or injuries to persons or property caused by or resulting from the acts or omissions of either party, their agents, servants or employees in the operation or maintenance of the dwelling unit or the premises of which it is a part; or
5. agrees to the establishment of a lien except as allowed by this act in and to the property of the other party.

If the lease contains such a provision, that provision is deemed *unenforceable*.

Flood problems – If the premises to be rented has been flooded within the past five (5) years and such fact is known to the landlord, the landlord shall include such information prominently and in writing as part of any written rental agreements. Failure to provide such information shall entitle any tenant who is a party to the rental agreement to sue the landlord of the premises in a court of appropriate jurisdiction and to recover the personal property damages sustained by the tenant from flooding of the premises.

Service animals – A landlord shall not deny or terminate a tenancy to a blind, deaf, or physically handicapped person because of the guide, signal, or service dog of such person.

Damage or security deposits – Any damage or security deposit required by a landlord of a tenant must be kept in an escrow account for the tenant, which account shall be maintained in the state of Oklahoma with a federally insured financial institution. Misappropriation of the security deposit shall be unlawful and punishable by a term in a county jail not to exceed six (6) months and by a fine in an amount not to exceed twice the amount misappropriated from the escrow account.

Upon termination of the tenancy, any security deposit held by the landlord may be applied to the payment of accrued rent and the amount of damages which the landlord has suffered by reason of the tenant's noncompliance with this act and the rental agreement, all as itemized by the landlord in a written statement delivered by mail to be by return receipt requested and to be signed for by any person of statutory service age at such address or in person to the tenant if he can reasonably be found. If the landlord proposes to retain any portion of the security deposit for rent, damages or other legally allowable charges under the provisions of this act or the rental agreement, the landlord shall return the balance of the security deposit without interest to the tenant within thirty (30) days after the termination of tenancy, delivery of possession and written demand by the tenant. If the tenant does not make such written demand of such deposit within six (6) months after termination of the tenancy, the deposit reverts to the landlord in consideration of the costs and burden of maintaining the escrow account, and the interest of the tenant in that deposit terminates at that time.

Serving notice and authorized landlords/managers – As a part of any rental agreement, the lessor shall prominently and in writing identify what person at what address is entitled to accept service or notice. The landlord or any person authorized to enter into a rental agreement on his behalf shall disclose to the tenant in writing at or before the commencement of the tenancy the name and address of:

1. the person or persons authorized to manage the premises;
2. the owner or owners of the premises; or
3. the name and address of a person authorized to act for and on behalf of the owner for the purpose of receipt of service of process and receiving and receipting for notices.

This information shall be kept current and this section extends to and is enforceable against any successor owner, landlord or manager.

Use – A rental agreement may provide reasonable limitations upon use of a dwelling unit or premises by a tenant or occupant. A landlord may adopt a rule concerning the tenant's use and occupancy of the premises which is enforceable against the tenant only if:

1. its purpose is to promote the convenience, peace, safety or welfare of the tenants in the premises, preserve the landlord's property from abusive use, or make a fair distribution of services and facilities held out for the tenants generally; and
2. it is reasonably related to the purpose for which it is adopted; and
3. it applies to all tenants in the premises in a fair manner; and
4. it is sufficiently explicit in its prohibition, direction or limitation of the tenant's conduct to fairly inform the tenant what such tenant must or must not do to comply; and
5. it is not for the purpose of evading the obligations of the landlord; and
6. the tenant has notice of it at the time such tenant enters into the rental agreement, or when it is adopted.

Demand to vacate – A landlord shall have the right to demand that an occupant vacate the dwelling premises if the occupant breaches any condition of the rental agreement which would be enforceable against the tenant. If a landlord makes a written request to the tenant or to an occupant for the occupant to depart from the dwelling, the occupant shall comply. If the occupant wrongfully fails to comply within a reasonable time, the occupant shall, upon conviction, be deemed guilty of a trespass and may be punished by a fine of not to exceed five hundred dollars ($500.00) or by confinement in the county jail for a period not to exceed thirty (30) days or by both such fine and imprisonment.

§118 identifies the duties of a landlord and of a tenant.

A. A **landlord** shall at all times during the tenancy:

1. Except in the case of a single-family residence, keep all common areas of his building, grounds, facilities and appurtenances in a clean, safe and sanitary condition;

2. Make all repairs and do whatever is necessary to put and keep the tenant's dwelling unit and premises in a fit and habitable condition;
3. Maintain in good and safe working order and condition all electrical, plumbing, sanitary, heating, ventilating, air-conditioning and other facilities and appliances, including elevators, supplied or required to be supplied by him;
4. Except in the case of one-or two-family residences or where provided by a governmental entity, provide and maintain appropriate receptacles and conveniences for the removal of ashes, garbage, rubbish and other waste incidental to the occupancy of the dwelling unit and arrange for the frequent removal of such wastes; and
5. Except in the case of a single-family residence or where the service is supplied by direct and independently-metered utility connections to the dwelling unit, supply running water and reasonable amounts of hot water at all times and reasonable heat.

§127 lists the duties of the **tenant.** The tenant shall at all times during the tenancy:

1. Keep that part of the premises which such tenant occupies and uses as safe, clean and sanitary as the condition of the premises permits;
2. Dispose from such tenant's dwelling unit all ashes, garbage, rubbish and other waste in a safe, clean and sanitary manner;
3. Keep all plumbing fixtures in the dwelling unit or used by the tenant as clean and sanitary as their condition permits;
4. Use in a safe and nondestructive manner all electrical, plumbing, sanitary, heating, ventilating, air-conditioning and other facilities and appliances including elevators in the premises;
5. Not deliberately or negligently destroy, deface, damage, impair or remove any part of the premises or permit any person, animal or pet to do so;
6. Not engage in conduct or allow any person or animal or pet, on the premises with the express or implied permission or consent of the tenant, to engage in conduct that will disturb the quiet and peaceful enjoyment of the premises by other tenants;
7. Comply with all covenants, rules, regulations and the like which are in accordance with Section 126 of this title; and
8. Not engage in criminal activity that threatens the health, safety or right of peaceful enjoyment of the premises by other tenants or is a danger to the premises, and not engage in any drug-related criminal activity on or near the premises either personally or by any member of the tenant's household or any guest or other person under the tenant's control.

Change of ownership – Upon termination of the owner's interest in the dwelling unit including, but not limited to, termination of interest by sale, assignment, death, bankruptcy, appointment of a receiver or otherwise, the *owner* is relieved of all liability under the rental agreement and of all obligations under the Act. The successor in interest to the owner shall then be liable for all obligations. Similarly, a property manager of the premises is relieved of liability under a rental agreement as to events occurring after written notice to the tenant of the termination of the management agreement.

Failure to deliver possession – If the landlord fails to deliver possession of the unit to the tenant, rent abates until possession is delivered and the tenant may terminate the rental agreement by giving a written notice of such termination to the landlord, whereupon the landlord shall return all prepaid rent and deposit, or the tenant may, at his option, demand performance of the rental agreement by the landlord and maintain an action for possession of the dwelling unit against any person wrongfully in possession and recover the actual damages sustained by him.

Non-compliance by the landlord – If there is a material noncompliance by the landlord with the terms of a rental agreement or the provisions of Section 118 of the Act which noncompliance materially affects health or safety, the tenant may deliver to the landlord a written notice specifying the acts and omissions constituting the breach and that the rental agreement will terminate upon a date not less than thirty (30) days after receipt of the notice if the breach is not remedied within fourteen (14) days, and thereafter the rental agreement shall so terminate.

If the breach is remediable by repairs, the reasonable cost of which is less than $100, the tenant may notify the landlord in writing of his intention to correct the condition at the landlord's expense after the expiration of fourteen (14) days. If the landlord fails to comply within said fourteen (14) days, or as promptly as conditions require in the case of an emergency, the tenant may thereafter cause the work to be done in a workmanlike manner and, after submitting to the landlord an itemized statement, deduct from his rent the actual and reasonable cost or the fair and reasonable value of the work.

If the landlord willfully or negligently fails to supply heat, running water, hot water, electric, gas or other essential service, the tenant may give written notice to the landlord specifying the breach and thereafter may:

1. upon written notice, immediately terminate the rental agreement; or
2. procure reasonable amounts of heat, hot water, running water, electric, gas or other essential service during the period of the landlord's noncompliance and deduct their actual and reasonable cost from the rent; or
3. recover damages based upon the diminution of the fair rental value of the dwelling unit; or
4. upon written notice, procure reasonable substitute housing during the period of the landlord's noncompliance, in which case the tenant is excused from paying rent for the period of the landlord's noncompliance.

If there is a noncompliance by the landlord which renders the dwelling unit uninhabitable or poses an imminent threat to the health and safety of any occupant, the tenant may immediately terminate the rental agreement upon written notice to the landlord which notice specifies the noncompliance.

Destruction of the property – If the property is damaged or destroyed by fire or other casualty to an extent that enjoyment of the dwelling unit is substantially impaired, unless the impairment is caused by the deliberate or negligent act or omission of the tenant, a member of his family, his animal or pet or other person or animal on the premises with his consent, the tenant may:

1. immediately vacate the premises and notify the landlord in writing within one (1) week thereafter of his intention to terminate the rental agreement, in which case the rental agreement terminates as of the date of vacating; or
2. if continued occupancy is possible, vacate any part of the dwelling unit rendered unusable by the fire or casualty, in which case the tenant's liability for rent is reduced in proportion to the diminution in the fair rental value of the dwelling unit.

If the rental agreement is terminated under this section, the landlord shall return all deposits recoverable and all prepaid and unearned rent.

Wrongful removal or exclusion – If a landlord wrongfully removes or excludes a tenant from possession of a dwelling unit, the tenant may recover possession by a proceeding brought in a court of competent jurisdiction, or terminate the rental agreement after giving notice of such intention to the landlord, and in either case recover an amount not more than twice the average monthly rental, or twice his actual damages, whichever is greater. If the rental agreement is terminated, the landlord shall return all deposits recoverable and all prepaid and unearned rent.

Unlawful or unreasonable entry – If the landlord makes an unlawful entry, or an entry in an unreasonable manner, or harasses the tenant by making repeated unreasonable demands for entry, the tenant may obtain injunctive relief to prevent the recurrence of the conduct or, upon written notice, terminate the rental agreement. In either case the tenant may recover actual damages.

However, a tenant shall not unreasonably withhold consent to the landlord, his agents and employees, to enter into the dwelling unit in order to inspect the premises, make necessary or agreed repairs, decorations, alterations or improvements, supply necessary or agreed services or exhibit the dwelling unit to prospective or actual purchasers, mortgagee, tenants, workmen or contractors.

A landlord, his agents and employees may enter the dwelling unit without consent of the tenant in case of emergency.

A landlord shall not abuse the right of access or use it to harass the tenant. Except in case of emergency, or unless it is impracticable to do so, the landlord shall give the tenant at least one (1) days' notice of his intent to enter and may enter only at reasonable times. Unless the tenant has abandoned or surrendered the premises, a landlord has no other right of access during a tenancy.

If the tenant refuses to allow lawful access, the landlord may obtain injunctive relief to compel access or he may terminate the rental agreement.

Wrongful abandonment – If the tenant wrongfully quits and abandons the dwelling unit during the term of the tenancy, the landlord shall make reasonable efforts to make the dwelling unit available for rental. If the landlord rents the dwelling unit for a term beginning before the expiration of the rental agreement, the existing rental agreement terminates as of the commencement date of the new tenancy. If the landlord fails to use reasonable efforts to make the dwelling unit available for rental, or if the landlord accepts the abandonment as a surrender,

the rental agreement is deemed to be terminated by the landlord as of the date the landlord has notice of the abandonment. If, after making reasonable efforts to make the dwelling unit available for rental after the abandonment, the landlord fails to re-rent the premises for a fair rental during the term, the tenant shall be liable for the entire rent or the difference in rental, whichever may be appropriate, for the remainder of the term.

Disposition of personal property – If the tenant abandons or surrenders possession, or is evicted, and leaves household goods, furnishings, fixtures, or any other personal property in the dwelling unit, the landlord may take possession of the property, and if, in the judgment of the landlord, the property has no ascertainable or apparent value, the landlord may dispose of the property without any duty of accounting or any liability to any party.

If, in the judgment of the landlord, the property has an ascertainable or apparent value, the landlord shall provide written notice to the tenant by certified mail to the last-known address that if the property is not removed within the time specified in the notice, the property will be deemed abandoned. Any property left with the landlord for a period of thirty (30) days or longer shall be conclusively determined to be abandoned and as such the landlord may dispose of said property in any manner which he deems reasonable and proper without liability to the tenant or any other interested party.

The landlord shall store all personal property of the tenant in a place of safekeeping and shall exercise reasonable care of the property. The landlord shall not be responsible to the tenant for any loss not caused by the landlord's deliberate or negligent act. The landlord may elect to store the property in the dwelling unit that was abandoned or surrendered by the tenant, in which event the storage cost may not exceed the fair rental value of the premises. If the tenant's property is removed to a commercial storage company, the storage cost shall include the actual charge for the storage and removal from the premises to the place of storage.

If the tenant removes the personal property within the time limitation, the landlord is entitled to the cost of storage for the period during which the property remained in the landlord's safekeeping plus all other costs that accrued under the rental agreement.

§130.1 "New Law" – The tenant shall:

1. provide the landlord with the name, address, and telephone number of a person to contact in the event of the tenant's death; and

2. sign a statement authorizing the landlord in the event of the tenant's death to:
   a. grant to the person designated access to the premises at a reasonable time and in the presence of the landlord or the landlord's agent,
   b. allow the person designated to remove any of the tenant's property found at the leased premises, and
   c. refund the tenant's security deposit, less lawful deductions, to the person designated

In the event of the death of a tenant who is the sole occupant of a rental dwelling:

1. the landlord may remove and store all property found in the tenant's leased premises;
2. the landlord shall turn over possession of the property to the person who was designated by the tenant or to any other person lawfully entitled to the property if the request is made prior to the property being discarded;
3. the landlord shall refund the tenant's security deposit, less lawful deductions, including the cost of removing and storing the property, to the person designated or to any other person lawfully entitled to the refund;
4. any person who removes property from the tenant's leased premises shall sign an inventory of the property being removed at the time of removal and submit the signed inventory to the landlord; and
5. the landlord may discard the property removed by the landlord from the tenant's leased premises if:

   a. the landlord has mailed a written request by certified mail, return receipt requested, to the person designated requesting that the property be removed,
   b. the person failed to remove the property by the thirtieth day after the postmark date of the notice, and
   c. the landlord, prior to the date of discarding the property, has not been contacted by anyone claiming the property.

If a tenant fails to provide the required information and statement, the landlord shall have no responsibility after the tenant's death for removal, storage, disappearance, damage, or disposition of property in the tenant's leased premises.

Delinquent rent – If rent is unpaid when due, the landlord may bring an action for recovery of the rent at any time thereafter or the landlord may wait until the expiration of the period allowed for curing a default by the tenant. A landlord may terminate a rental agreement for failure to pay rent when due, if the tenant fails to pay rent within five (5) days after written notice of landlord's demand for payment. The notice may be given before or after the landlord files any action. Demand for past due rent is deemed a demand for possession of the premises and no further notice to quit possession need be given by the landlord to the tenant for any purpose.

Noncompliance by the tenant – Noncompliance by the tenant which can be remedied by repair, replacement of a damaged item, or cleaning, and the tenant fails to comply as promptly as conditions require in the case of an emergency or within ten (10) days after written notice served by the landlord specifying the breach and requiring that the tenant remedy it within that period of time, the landlord may enter the dwelling unit and cause the work to be done in a workmanlike manner and thereafter submit the itemized bill for the actual and reasonable cost or the fair and reasonable value thereof as rent on the next date rent is due, or if the rental agreement has terminated, for immediate payment. If the landlord remedies the breach, the landlord may not terminate the rental agreement by reason of the tenant's failure to remedy the breach.

If there is a material noncompliance by the tenant, the landlord may deliver to the tenant a written notice served specifying the acts and omissions constituting the noncompliance and that the rental agreement will terminate upon a date not less than fifteen (15) days after receipt of the notice unless remedied within ten (10) days. If the breach is not remedied within ten (10) days from receipt of the notice, the rental agreement shall terminate as provided in the notice. If within the ten (10) days the tenant adequately remedies the breach complained of, or if the landlord remedies the breach, the rental agreement shall not terminate by reason of the breach. Any subsequent breach of the lease or noncompliance under this section shall be grounds, upon written notice to the tenant, for immediate termination of the lease.

If there is a noncompliance by the tenant that causes or threatens to cause imminent and irremediable harm to the premises or to any person and which noncompliance is not remedied by the tenant as promptly as conditions require after the tenant has notice of it, the landlord may terminate the rental agreement by immediately filing a forcible entry and detainer action.

Any criminal activity that threatens the health, safety or right of peaceful enjoyment of the premises by other tenants committed by a tenant or by any member of the tenant's household or any guest or other person under the tenant's control or is a danger to the premises and any drug related criminal activity on or near the premises by the tenant or by any member of the tenant's household or any guest or other person under the tenant's control shall be grounds for immediate termination of the lease.

The remaining few pages of this chapter contain the lease agreement as used in the Greater Tulsa Association of REALTORS®. Reading the document will give the student further comprehension of the topics covered throughout the chapter.

This is a legally binding Contract; if not understood seek advice from an attorney.

SINGLE FAMILY RESIDENCE OR CONDOMINIUM LEASE

Owner_____

Tenant(s)_____ (the "Tenant")

Owner's Broker _____. a licensed real estate broker

Premises_____ City_____ State____ Zip_____

In consideration of their mutual agreement to the following terms, conditions, and covenants, the Owner/Owner's Broker leases to Tenant and Tenant leases from Owner/Owner's Broker the above described Premises.

TERMS, CONDITIONS AND COVENANTS

1. **TERM.** This Lease commences on_____("Commencement Date") and expires on _____("Expiration Date"). Any extension of the "Expiration Date" must be mutually agreed upon in writing prior to the "Expiration Date." Tenant agrees to give Owner/Owner's Broker written notice of intent to terminate the lease, or request to extend the lease, at least 30-days, but no more than 45-days prior to the "Expiration Date."

2. **RENT.** Rental Rate shall be $ _____ per month and is payable in advance on the first day of each and

    every calendar month and shall be paid to _____

    Address: _____ .

    Prorated rent in the amount of $_____ for the month of _____ is

    payable on or before _____ .

    a) **Late Payment of Rent Fee.** Any rent payment that is not received by Owner's Broker by 12:01 a.m. on the _____ day of the month it is due will be assessed a late fee of _____. Total amount of rent and late fee is to be paid by money order, cashiers check or other certified funds.

    b) **Deductions from Rent.** Deductions made from rents without written permission from Owner/Owner's Broker will be considered as unpaid rent and will subject Tenant to a late fee.

    c) **Dishonored Checks.** In the event that Tenant's check is returned by the bank for any reason (insufficient funds, stopped payment, etc.), **Tenant agrees:**

        1) To replace the returned check with a cashier's check or money order within twenty-four (24) hours. Dishonored checks will not be re-deposited.

        2) To include payment of $_____ dishonored check charge with the replacement cashier's check or money order along with applicable late charges.

        3) If Tenant has a second dishonored check, Tenant shall pay all further rents with cashier's check or money order.

    d) **Five Day Notice to Evict.** In the case of non-payment of rent or tendering a dishonored check, a five-day (5) notice to "move or suffer eviction" shall be given as allowed by law.

3. **POSSESSION OF PREMISES.** Tenant acknowledges that the statements and material representations made on Tenant's signed application, which is hereby incorporated by reference, have been relied upon by Owner/Owner's Broker, the falsity of which, in whole or in part, shall constitute a breach of this lease entitling Owner/Owner's Broker at Owner's/Owner's Broker's option, to terminate the lease and repossess the premises. This lease is further conditioned upon Owner/Owner's Broker securing possession of the premises from the existing Tenant, if any, by the commencement date hereof. In the event Owner or Owner's Broker is unable to deliver possession of the premises to Tenant for any reason, including, but not limited to, failure of previous Tenant to vacate Premises or partial or complete destruction of the Premises, Tenant shall have the right to terminate this Agreement. In such event, Owner's

_____   _____
Tenant's Initials   Owner's/Owner's Broker Initials

Single Family Residence or Condominium Lease Continued

or Owner's Broker's liability shall be limited to the return of all sums previously paid by Tenant to Owner/Owner's Broker except application processing fee, if any.

4. **LEGAL USE.** Tenant shall use the Leased Premises only for residential purposes and for no other purpose. Operating a business, including daycare, from this property is prohibited. Tenant shall not use, nor permit the use of anything in the Leased Premises (i) which would violate any of the agreements in this Lease, (ii) for any unlawful purpose or in any unlawful manner, or (iii) that would substantially increase cost of the Landlord's insurance. Tenant shall comply with City Code and Ordinances, City, State and Federal Regulations and Laws. Tenant shall pay any cost incurred by Owner/Owner's Broker due to Tenant's violation of such Code, Regulations, Ordinances and Laws and Tenant's violation shall constitute a breach of this Lease Agreement.

5. **SECURITY DEPOSIT.** Tenant shall deposit with Owner/Owner's Broker a Security Deposit in the amount of _____ ($_____) upon execution of this Agreement. This Security Deposit shall secure the performance of Tenant's obligations hereunder including leaving the Premises in the same condition as they were received, normal wear and tear excepted. Tenant shall provide Owner/Owner's Broker a written list of defects and/or items in need of repair within two (2) weeks after occupancy. Owner/Owner's Broker may, but shall not be obligated to apply the security deposit or any portion thereof to Tenant's obligations hereunder. Any balance remaining upon termination shall be returned to Tenant within thirty (30) days of both the Tenant giving written request for the return of the deposit and the Tenant giving possession of the Premises to the Owner/Owner's Broker. Tenant shall **NOT** have the right to apply the Security Deposit for payment of rent. If any money is withheld from the deposit, the Owner/Owner's Broker shall provide Tenant with an itemized list of expenses withheld. Owner/Owner's Broker shall deposit the Security Deposit in an FDIC insured escrow account. Such account may bear interest, which shall be payable to Owner's Broker in consideration of the cost and burden of maintaining the escrow account.

6. **PETS.** Tenant shall not keep pets of any kind (except trained dogs needed by blind, deaf or physically disabled persons) on the Premises without prior permission from the Owner/Owner's Broker. If permission is granted, (as indicated in the application), Tenant agrees to pay the cost of having the Premises treated, if needed, by a professional exterminator and carpets professionally cleaned at the termination of occupancy, and Tenant agrees to maintain such pet on the Premises only so long as permitted by Owner/Owner's Broker. **If, after move-in, a pet is acquired without written permission of Owner/Owner's Broker an eviction notice will be issued.**

7. **UTILITIES.** Utilities must be in Tenant's name on the Lease "Commencement Date." Utilities shall not be turned off until the Tenant has notified Owner/Owner's Broker of move out date, vacated the property, turned in the keys and has fulfilled all obligations of this Lease Agreement.

8. **OCCUPANTS.** Premises shall be occupied only by the persons listed below. Occupancy by anyone other than those listed for more than fourteen (14) consecutive nights shall constitute a breach of this Agreement unless prior consent is given in writing by Owner/Owner's Broker:

_____

_____

9. **MAINTENANCE.** Owner agrees to maintain the dwelling, all appliances furnished, mechanical equipment, plumbing and electrical facilities in or on the Premises at the commencement of this lease.

    Exceptions:_____

Tenant agrees to be responsible for repairs needed due to misuse.

10. **ALTERATIONS AND REPAIRS.** Except in the event of an emergency, no repairs, decorating or alterations shall be done by Tenant without Owner's/Owner's Broker's prior written consent. Tenant shall notify Owner/Owner's Broker in writing of any repairs or alterations contemplated. Tenant shall hold Owner and Owner's Broker harmless as to any mechanic's lien recordation or proceeding caused by Tenant and Tenant agrees to indemnify Owner and Owner's Broker in the event of any such claim or proceeding. Tenant agrees that all improvements installed in and on the Premises, including landscaping (bushes, shrubs, ground cover, trees, and flowers) shall, at the option of Owner/

Tenant's Initials	Owner's/Owner'sBroker Initials

Single Family Residence or Condominium Lease Continued

Owner's Broker, remain with the Premises upon termination of the Lease at no cost to Owner or Owner's Broker.

11. **APPLICATION OF FUNDS.** Money paid by Tenant shall be applied in the following order.

    a) Maintenance charges due in accordance with Paragraph 12 *"Tenant's Responsibilities for the Care of the Premises"* and Paragraph 13 *"Tenant's Responsibilities for Maintenance."*
    b) Late charges, dishonored check charges, or trip charges.
    c) Past due utilities.
    d) Unpaid security deposits.
    e) Attorney fees, Processor fees, and Court Costs
    f) Past due rent, oldest month to newest.
    g) Current rent

12. **TENANT'S RESPONSIBILITIES FOR THE CARE OF THE PREMISES.** Tenant shall be responsible for the following items and for other Tenant damage not listed below:

    a) Keep the Premises clean and sanitary inside and out, and in good order and condition.
    b) Watering, mowing, edging, trimming shrubs and weeding flowerbeds as required for proper care and maintenance.
    Exceptions_____
    c) Neither mar nor deface the walls, woodwork or any part of the Premises.
    d) Immediately report to Owner/Owner's Broker those items needing repair.
    e) Pay Owner/Owner's Broker upon demand for damage to Premises as a result of failure to report a problem in a timely manner.
    f) Pay Owner/Owner's Broker upon demand for cost to repair, replace or rebuild any portion of the Premises damaged whether through act or negligence by the Tenant, Tenant's guests, or invitees.
    g) Pay Owner/Owner's Broker upon demand for damage caused by rain or wind as a result of leaving windows or doors open, or lawn hoses left connected outside resulting in freezing damage.
    h) A telephone is required and Tenant shall have telephone service within fourteen (14) days of occupancy and furnish Owner/Owner's Broker with the telephone number and notify Owner/Owner's Broker of any telephone number changes. Should it be necessary for Owner/Owner's Broker to drive to the Premises for any reason due to Tenant not having a telephone, Tenant agrees to pay a _____ dollar ($_____) trip charge. Tenant shall also be responsible for cost of repairing telephone lines damaged by the Tenant.
    i) If Tenant changes locks, Tenant shall furnish keys to Owner or Owner's Broker within five (5) days or pay the cost of a locksmith to make a set of keys. All keys and garage door openers must be returned the day of vacating the Premises. If Tenant fails to return said keys and garage door openers (in working order), Tenant agrees to pay the cost to re-key the Premises and to the replace garage door openers.

13. **TENANT'S RESPONSIBILITIES FOR MAINTENANCE.** Tenant shall be responsible for the following:

    a) Vacuuming carpet on a regular basis.
    b) Changing the furnace/air-conditioner filter at least once every two (2) months.
    c) Replacing burned out light bulbs, regular or fluorescent.
    d) Any breakage, damage, destruction and/or soiling caused by acts of the Tenant or by Tenant's employees, agents, visitors or pets. In the event of vandalism, break-ins, or broken glass, Tenant agrees to pay all repair cost, regardless of the circumstances of breakage, unless Tenant, at Tenant's expense, supplies Owner/Owner's Broker with a copy of a police report.
    e) Tenant agrees that smoking in the premises is not permitted and should cigarette smoke damage occur due to Tenant, Tenant's employees, or Tenant's visitors smoking within the dwelling, Tenant agrees to pay the cost of having premises painted, walls washed, interior deodorized and carpets and draperies professionally cleaned, and any other cost to repair smoke damage.
    f) Exterminating ants, rodents, fleas, cockroaches, spiders, and other insects and pests.
    g) Use plunger on clogged toilets and drains before calling Owner/Owner's Broker.
    h) Pay Owner/Owner's Broker upon demand for unnecessary workman service calls.
    i) Under no circumstances is Tenant to perform any electrical, gas line, or water line repairs.

                                  _____   _____
                                    Tenant's Initials   Owner's/Owner'sBroker Initials

Single Family Residence or Condominium Lease Continued

j) Tenant agrees to pay a $_____ trip charge in the event a breach of this Lease Agreement by Tenant (i.e., failure to pay rent, dishonored check, unauthorized pet, failure to maintain landscaping, etc.) requires a trip to the Premises by Owner/Owner's Broker.

14. **ASSIGNMENT AND SUBLETTING.** No portion of the Premises shall be sublet nor this Agreement assigned. Any attempted subletting or assignment by Tenant, at the option of the Owner, shall be a breach of this Agreement.

15. **MOTOR VEHICLES, BOATS, ETC.** No more than _____ motor vehicles may be kept on or near the Premises. No motor coach, trailer, camper, boat or other recreational vehicles shall be parked on or near the Premises. No commercial vehicles in excess of ¾ ton may be parked on or near the Premises. Tenant shall not perform vehicular repairs on, in, or in front of Premises.

   Vehicles shall not be parked, repaired, or washed on the lawn. Vehicles leaking fluids, oil, brake fluid, transmission fluid, gasoline, and batteries shall not be allowed on the Premises. Inoperative and unregistered vehicles shall not be parked on, in, or in front of Premises. Tenant agrees to pay for towing of any vehicle that is in violation of this paragraph.

16. **INSURANCE.** All personal property located on or stored in the Premises shall be kept and stored at Tenant's sole risk and Tenant shall indemnify and hold harmless Owner and Owner's Broker from and against any loss or damage to such property arising from any cause whatsoever. **Further, Tenant is responsible for obtaining Tenant's own insurance to cover Tenant's personal property and liability as Owner shall only carry insurance on the dwelling.**

17. **INVENTORY.** The following items are included in the dwelling unit: Carpet, range, oven, disposal, dishwasher, window coverings. Other items included, if any _____

   _____

18. **ENTRY AND INSPECTION.** Owner and Owner's Broker, in accordance with state law, shall have the right to enter the Premises: (a) in case of emergency; (b) to make necessary or agreed repairs, or supply necessary or agreed service, (c) exhibit the Premises to prospective or actual purchasers, mortgagees, tenants, workmen, and contractors; (d) when Tenant has abandoned or surrendered the Premises. Except under (a) and (d), entry shall be made only during normal business hours, and not less than one (1) day prior notice shall be given to Tenant. Notwithstanding the provisions of Paragraph 21 below, for the purpose of entry and inspection, notice may be posted on the Premises.

19. **ATTORNEY'S FEES.** In the event legal action or proceeding is brought by either party to enforce any part of this Lease Agreement, the prevailing party shall recover, in addition to all other relief, reasonable attorney's fees and costs.

20. **CONDOMINIUMS.** It is recommended that Tenant read the Condominium Rules and Regulations. Tenant agrees to pay, upon demand, any fines levied upon Owner for Tenant's violation of the condominium rules and regulations. Tenant is responsible for maintaining working light bulbs in front/rear porch and carport light fixtures.

21. **NOTICE.** Notice to Owner may be served to Owner's Broker at the following address:_____

   _____. Owner's Broker is authorized to accept legal service on behalf of Owner. Any notice provided for or permitted by this Lease to be given by one party to the other, may be given sufficiently for all purposes in writing, mailed as certified United States mail, postage prepaid, addressed to Owner's Broker (or Tenant) to be notified at Owner's Broker's (or Tenant's) address as set forth herein in writing, or delivered personally to Owner's Broker (or Tenant), and shall be deemed conclusively to have been given on the date of such mailing or personal delivery.

22. **SURRENDER.** Tenant agrees that upon vacating the premises to surrender the Premises and all fixtures and equipment of Owner therein in good, clean and operating condition, ordinary wear and tear excepted. Tenant shall at the time of vacating the premises, thoroughly clean the Premises, including, but not limited to, all appliances, removal of all trash from the Premises and shall pay for the cost of Owner/Owner's Broker having the carpet professionally cleaned. Further, upon vacating the Property, Tenant shall secure the property and immediately deliver all keys and

....
Tenant's Initials   Owner's/Owner's Broker Initials

garage door openers, if any, to Owner/Owner's Broker as set out in paragraph 12(i) of this Lease. If such cleaning and removal of trash is not accomplished by Tenant, action deemed necessary by Owner/Owner's Broker to accomplish same may be taken by Owner/Owner's Broker at Tenant's expense. If Tenant fails to secure the property and return all keys and garage door openers (if any), Tenant agrees to pay any cost incurred by the Owner/Owner's Broker to secure the Property including any repairs for damage to the Property as the result of the Tenant's failure to secure the Property, and/or replace keys, locks and garage door openers.

23. **BREACH OF CONTRACT.** In the event of default by any one signatory, each and every remaining signatory shall be liable for timely payment of rent and shall be bound by all the terms, conditions and covenants of this Lease Agreement whether or not in actual possession of the premises. Should Tenant neglect or fail to perform and observe any of the terms of this Lease, Owner/Owner's Broker shall give Tenant written notice of such breach, delivered to Tenant personally or mailed by certified mail, requiring the Tenant to immediately remedy the breach or vacate the Premises on or before a date at least fifteen (15) days after date of the notice (except in the event such breach is for failure to pay rent in which case the five (5) day statutory notice shall apply). If Tenant fails to comply with such notice the Owner/Owner's Broker may declare this Lease terminated and institute action to evict Tenant from the premises without limiting the liability of Tenant for rent due or to become due under this Lease. In the event of a breach of this Agreement or eviction of Tenant for breach of this Agreement, Tenant agrees to pay Owner/ Owner's Broker for all losses incurred as the result of such breach and/or eviction, including, but not limited to attorney's fees, late fees, rent, advertising costs, cleaning, painting, repairs, landscaping, etc., and re-letting expense of _____% of one month's rent.

24. **WAIVER BY OWNER.** The waiver by Owner/Owner's Broker of any breach shall not be construed to be a continuing waiver of any subsequent breach. The receipt by the Owner/Owner's Broker of the rent with the knowledge of any violation of a covenant or condition hereto shall not be deemed a waiver of such breach. No waiver by Owner/Owner's Broker of the provisions herein shall be deemed to have been made unless expressed in writing and signed by Owner or Owner's Broker.

25. **DISCLOSURES.**

   a) **Lead-Based Paint (Applicable to Property built before 1978 ONLY).** Tenant acknowledges that prior to signing this Lease, Tenant received the Owner's completed and signed **"Disclosure of Information on Lead-Based Paint and Lead-Based Paint Hazards"** and Tenant has received and read a copy of the **EPA** *Protect Your Family From Lead in Your Home* pamphlet, which explains the hazards of lead-based paint.

   b) **Flood Zone.** The Owner here by discloses the following flood hazard information: The above described Premises _____ is _____ is not located within a flood hazard area as indicated on Flood Insurance Rate Maps. In the event the property is located in a flood hazard area, Tenant acknowledges that Tenant has received, read and signed the **"Notice to Tenant of Location in Flood Hazard Area."**

   c) **Broker Relationship Disclosure.** Tenant and Owner acknowledge that prior to signing this Lease Agreement, they received and read a copy of the *For Lease for Tenants and Landlords* guide prepared by the Greater Tulsa Association of REALTORS, which includes an explanation of the Broker relationships. Tenant and Owner further acknowledge that prior to signing this Lease, the following disclosures were made to each of them:

   _____(Owner's Broker) is acting

   ☐ as a Single-Party Broker for the Owner   ☐ as a Transaction Broker for the Owner

   ☐ as a Single-Party Broker for Tenant   ☐ as a Transaction Broker for the Tenant

   ☐ as a Transaction Broker for both the Owner and the Tenant

   _____   _____
   Tenant's Initials   Owner's/Owner'sBroker Initials

Single Family Residence or Condominium Lease Continued

_____ (Locating Broker) is acting

☐ as a Single-Party Broker for the Owner   ☐ as a Single-Party Broker of the Tenant

☐ as a Transaction Broker for the Owner   ☐ as a Transaction Broker of the Tenant

☐ as a Transaction Broker for both the Owner and the Tenant

    d) Fair Housing. Owner, Owner's Broker and Tenant acknowledge and agree that Owner/Owner's Broker shall lease the Premises to the Tenant without regard to sex, race, religion, color, handicap, familial status, or national origin.

26. **ENTIRE AGREEMENT.** This Lease Agreement constitutes the entire Agreement between the parties, and no promises or representations, other than those contained herein, have been made by Owner or Owner's Broker. Any modifications to this Agreement must be in writing and signed by Owner or Owner's Broker and Tenant.

27. **OTHER CONDITIONS.** _____

_____

_____

_____

_____

_____

_____

_____

28. **SMOKE DETECTORS.** Tenant agrees to test the smoke detector at least once a week. If the detector is battery powered, Tenant agrees to replace the battery as needed. After replacing the battery, if the smoke detector still does not work, Tenant agrees to inform Owner or Owner's Broker immediately in writing. If the detector is not battery powered, Tenant agrees to inform Owner or Owner's Broker immediately of any malfunction. Tenant has been instructed on the care and operation of the smoke detector and knows how to operate and care for the smoke detector.

29. **CARBON MONOXIDE DETECTORS.** Tenant is authorized to install a carbon monoxide detector. If detector is battery operated, Tenant agrees to test such detector once a week and replace batteries as needed.

30. **ADDENDUMS.** Tenant has received the following attachments and addendums, if any, which by reference are hereby incorporated in and made a part of this Lease:

_____

THE UNDERSIGNED Tenant(s) acknowledges having read and understood the above and has received a copy of this Lease Agreement and all attachments and addendums and accepts the Property in its present condition.

Tenant : _____   Date _____

Tenant: _____   Date _____

Owner/Owner'sBroker: _____   Date _____

By: _____   Date _____
              Owner's Broker

CHAPTER 3:

Property Management and the Nonresidential/Residential Landlord and Tenant Acts
End of Chapter Quiz

1. Most property management agreements include all of the following information, EXCEPT:

    a. the manager's scope of authority
    b. reporting requirements
    c. conditions for termination of the agreement
    d. the marketing methods to be utilized

2. An Oklahoma residential lease, which created a month-to-month tenancy, requires one party to provide notice of intent to terminate the agreement to the other at least:

    a. seven days before the date upon which the termination is to become effective.
    b. 30 days before the date upon which the termination is to become effective.
    c. 60 days before the date upon which the termination is to become effective.
    d. No notice is required.

3. A tenant who wrongfully remains in possession without the landlord's consent after the expiration of the term of the rental agreement is said to create a(n):

    a. holdover tenancy.
    b. estate at sufferance.
    c. stay of execution.
    d. estate at will.

4. Oklahoma leases may *not* contain any of the following provisions EXCEPT that either party:

    a. agrees to pay the other party's attorney's fees.
    b. agrees to the indemnification of any liability arising for damages or injuries resulting from the acts of the other party.
    c. agrees to reserve the right to assign or sub-lease to another party.
    d. agrees to the establishment of a lien to the property of the other party.

5. Which of the following is FALSE regarding security deposits held by an Oklahoma landlord?

    a. Deposits must be kept in an escrow account for the tenant.
    b. Escrow accounts must be maintained in the state of Oklahoma with a federally insured financial institution.
    c. Misappropriation of the security deposits shall be punishable by a term in a county jail not to exceed six (6) months.
    d. Misappropriation of the security deposits may be punishable by a fine up to $5,000.

6. A tenant who breaches any condition of the rental agreement, which is followed by the landlord's demand for the tenant to vacate who then wrongfully fails to comply:

   a. shall be guilty of a trespass.
   b. may be punished by a fine up to $500.
   c. may be punished by up to 30 days in jail
   d. all of these

7. Duties imposed upon the tenant in an Oklahoma residential tenancy include all of these *EXCEPT*:

   a. permit and accommodate showings to future, prospective tenants who express an interest in seeing the property.
   b. maintain the premises in a safe, clean and sanitary condition.
   c. use all mechanical equipment, facilities, and appliances in a safe and responsible manner.
   d. not deliberately or negligently destroy, deface, damage, impair, or remove any part of the premises or permit anyone else to do so.

8. An Oklahoma landlord may enter into the dwelling unit under all of the following circumstances *EXCEPT*:

   a. in order to inspect the premises or make necessary repairs with proper notice.
   b. any time the tenant is delinquent with the payment of rent.
   c. without consent of the tenant in case of emergency.
   d. provided the landlord give the tenant at least one days' notice.

9. Which of these is *TRUE* regarding the disposition of personal property left behind in a leased dwelling?

   a. If the tenant abandons personal property in the dwelling unit, the landlord may *not* take possession of the personal property under any condition.
   b. If, in the judgment of the landlord, the property has no apparent value, the landlord may dispose of the property without liability.
   c. Any property left with the landlord for a period of 90 days or longer shall be conclusively determined to be abandoned and may be disposed of in any manner.
   d. If the landlord stores the tenant's property with a commercial storage company, and the tenant wishes to claim the property, the landlord is *not* entitled to reimbursement for the cost of storage.

10. The "New Law" §130.1, requires:

    a. the tenant to provide the landlord
       with contact information of a
       designated person in the event of
       the tenant's death.
    b. the person designated to remove
       any of the tenant's property
       found at the leased premises.
    c. the refund of the tenant's security
       deposit, less lawful deductions, to
       the person designated.
    d. all of these

Chapter 4
Residential Property Condition Disclosure Statement; Residential Property Condition Disclaimer Statement

As we said in the national portion of this course, most states mandate that the seller disclose property conditions or defects associated with the property which adversely affects its use or value. This form is a "standardized condition form" and has a variety of names in a variety of states. In Oklahoma, it is called a Residential Property Disclosure Statement and most of this chapter is devoted to the Act and the form. The unit also addresses the Residential Property Disclaimer Statement.

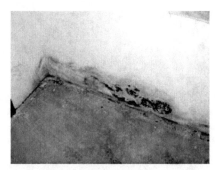

DO YOU KNOW???

Do you know what a licensee must do and must not do to be in compliance with the *Residential Property Condition Disclosure Act?*

Are you aware of the remedies available to the purchaser if the seller should fail to comply?

Can you explain the circumstances under which a seller would use the *Residential Property Disclaimer Statement?*

These are just some of the topics to be covered in this chapter.

THE ACT

The *Residential Property Condition Disclosure Act*, Title 60, O.S., Sections 831 et. seq., effective July 1, 1995, requires sellers of one or two residential dwelling units to complete the *Residential Property Condition Disclosure Statement*. The seller must complete, sign, and date this disclosure and deliver it to the purchaser *as soon as practicable*, but in any event *no later than before an offer is accepted by the seller*. If the seller becomes aware of a defect after delivery of this statement, but before the seller accepts an offer to purchase, the seller must deliver an amended disclosure statement disclosing the newly discovered defect.

The document states that the information contained in the disclosure statement are not warranties, express or implied of any kind, and are not a substitute for any inspections or warranties the purchaser may wish to obtain. The information and statements contained in the disclosure statement are declarations and representations of the seller and are not representations of any licensee.

The following verbiage was taken directly from the Oklahoma Residential Property Disclosure Act:

Preface

The Oklahoma Real Estate Commission does not have jurisdiction over the Residential Property Condition Disclosure Act but does have jurisdiction over a real estate licensee who fails to comply with this act.

The Real Estate Commission is responsible for developing and amending the disclosure and disclaimer forms and making such forms available.

This pamphlet has been compiled and published for the benefit of real estate licensees and members of the general public for information purposes only. It is intended as a general guide and is not for the purpose of answering specific legal questions. Questions of interpretation should be referred to an attorney.

Any alleged dispute or violation of this Act of a civil nature must be adjudicated in a court of proper jurisdiction. Further, if the violation involves a real estate licensee, individuals should contact the Real Estate Commission.

Oklahoma Real Estate commission
Shepherd Mall
2401 N.W. 23rd Street, Suite 18
Oklahoma City, Oklahoma 73107-2431
www.orec.ok.gov
405-521-3387

The Residential Property Condition Disclosure Act
Oklahoma Statutes, Title 60, Sections 831-839 Section 831, Short title. This act shall be known and may be cited as the "Residential Property Condition Disclosure Act."

Section 832. Definitions As used in this act:
1. "Offer to purchase" means an offer to purchase property made by a purchaser pursuant to a written contract;
2. "Seller" means one or more persons who are attempting to transfer a possessory interest in property and who are either:
    a.   represented by a real estate licensee; or
    b.   not represented by a real estate licensee but receive a written request from the purchaser to deliver or cause to be delivered a disclaimer statement or disclosure statement as such terms are defined in paragraphs 11 and 12 of this section.
3. "Purchaser" means one or more persons who are attempting to acquire a possessory interest in property;
4. "Real estate licensee" means a person licensed under the Oklahoma Real Estate License Code;
5. "Transfer" means a sale or conveyance, exchange or option to purchase by written instrument of a possessory interest in property for consideration;
6. "Person" means an individual, corporation, limited liability company, partnership, association, trust or other legal entity or any combination thereof;
7. "Contract" means a real estate purchase contract for the sale, conveyance or exchange of property, option to purchase property, or a lease with an option to purchase property;
8. "Property" means residential real property improved with not less than one nor more than two dwelling units;

9. "Defect" means a condition, malfunction or problem that would have a materially adverse effect on the monetary value of the property, or that would impair the health or safety of future occupants of the property;

10. "Disclosure" means a written declaration required by this act based on actual knowledge of the seller regarding certain physical conditions of the property. a disclosure for purposes of this act is not a warranty, implied or express, of any kind;

11. "Disclaimer statement" means the statement described in paragraph 1 of subsection A of section 3 of this act; and

12. "Disclosure statement" means the statement described in paragraph 2 of subsection A of section 3 of this act.

Section 833. Disclaimer and disclosure statements

A. A seller of property located in this state shall deliver, or cause to be delivered, to the purchaser of such property one of the following:

1. A written property disclaimer statement on a form established by rule by the Oklahoma Real Estate Commission which states that the seller:

    a.   has never occupied the property and makes no disclosures concerning the condition of the property, and

    b.   has no actual knowledge of any defect; or

2. A written property condition disclosure statement on a form established by rule by the Oklahoma Real Estate Commission which shall include the information set forth in subsection B of this section.

B. 1. The disclosure statement shall include an identification of items and improvements which are included in the sale of the property and whether such items or improvements are in normal working order. The disclosures required shall also include a statement of whether the seller has actual knowledge of defects or information in relation to the following:

    a.   water and sewer systems, including the source of household water, water treatment systems, sprinkler systems, occurrence of water in the heating and air conditioning ducts, water seepage or leakage, drainage or grading problems and flood zone status,

    b.   structural systems, including the roof, walls, floors, foundation and any basement,

    c.   plumbing, electrical heating and air conditioning systems,

    d.   infestation or damage of wood-destroying organisms,

    e.   major fire or tornado damage,

    f.   land use matters,

    g.   existence of hazardous or regulated materials and other conditions having an environmental impact.

    h.   existence of prior manufacturing of methamphetamine,

    i.   any other defects known to the seller, and

    j.   other matters the Oklahoma Real Estate Commission deems appropriate.

2. The disclosure statement shall include the following notices to the purchaser in bold and conspicuous type:

    a.   "The information and statements contained in this disclosure statement are declarations and representations of the seller and are not the representations of the real estate licensee."

  b. "The information contained in this disclosure statement is not intended to be a part of any contract between the purchaser and the seller." and

  c. "The declarations and information contained in this disclosure statement are not warranties, express or implied of any kind, and are not a substitute for any inspections or warranties the purchaser may wish to obtain."

C. Either the disclaimer statement or the disclosure statement required by this section must be completed, signed and dated by the seller. The date of completion on either statement may not be more than one hundred eighty (180) days prior to the date of receipt for the statement by the purchaser.

D. The Oklahoma Real Estate Commission shall develop by rule the forms for the residential property condition disclaimer and the residential property condition disclosure statement. After development of the initial forms, the Oklahoma Real Estate Commission may amend by rule the forms as is necessary and appropriate. Such forms shall be made available upon request irrespective of whether the person requesting a disclaimer or disclosure form is represented by a real estate licensee.

Section 834. Delivery of statements

A. A seller should deliver either the disclaimer statement or disclosure statement to the purchaser as soon as practicable, but in any event it shall be delivered before acceptance of an offer to purchase.

B. If the disclaimer statement or disclosure statement is delivered to the purchaser after an offer to purchase has been made, the offer to purchase shall be accepted only after the purchaser has acknowledged receipt of the disclaimer statement or disclosure statement and confirmed the offer to purchase.

C. If the seller becomes aware of a defect after delivery to the purchaser of either a disclaimer statement or a disclosure statement, then the seller shall promptly deliver to the purchaser either a disclosure statement or an amended disclosure statement which discloses the newly discovered defect. The disclosure statement or any amendment shall be in writing and shall be signed and dated by the seller. However, if the required document is delivered to the purchaser after an offer to purchase has been made, the offer to purchase shall be accepted only after the purchaser has acknowledged receipt of the required document and confirmed the offer to purchase.

D. The purchaser shall acknowledge in writing receipt of the disclaimer statement or the disclosure statement and any amendment to the disclosure statement. The purchaser shall sign and date any acknowledgement. Such acknowledgement should accompany the offer to purchase the property. If the purchaser confirms the offer to purchase, such confirmation shall be in writing, shall be signed and dated by the purchaser and shall be promptly delivered to the seller.

Section 835. Limitation of seller's liability

A.   The seller shall not be liable for a defect or other condition in the property if the existence of the defect or other condition in the property was disclosed in the disclosure statement or any amendment delivered to the purchaser before acceptance of the offer to purchase.

B.   The seller shall not be liable for any erroneous, inaccurate or omitted information supplied to the purchaser as a disclosure required by this act if:

    1.   The error in accuracy or omission results from an approximation of information by the seller provided:

        a.   accurate information was unknown to the seller at the time the disclosure was made

        b.   the approximation was clearly identified as such and was reasonable and based on the best information available to the seller, and

        c.   the approximation was not used to circumvent the disclosure requirements of this act;

    2.   The error, inaccuracy or omission was not within the actual knowledge of the seller; or

    3.   The disclosure was based on information provided by public agencies and the seller reasonably believed the information to be correct.

C.   The delivery by a public agency of any information required to be disclosed by the seller of the property shall satisfy the requirements of this act as to the disclosures to which the information being furnished is applicable.

Section 836. Duties of real estate licensee

A.   A real estate licensee representing or assisting a seller has the duty to obtain from the seller a disclaimer statement or a disclosure statement and any amendment required by the Residential Property Condition Disclosure Act and to make such statement available to potential purchasers prior to acceptance of an offer to purchase.

B.   A real estate licensee representing or assisting a purchaser has the duty to obtain and make available to the purchaser a disclaimer statement or a disclosure statement and any amendment required by the Residential Property Condition Disclosure Act prior to the acceptance of an offer to purchase.

C.   A real estate licensee has the duty to disclose to the purchaser any defects in the property actually known to the licensee which are not included in the disclosure statement or any amendment.

D.   A real estate licensee who has complied with the requirements of subsections A, B and C of this section, as applicable, shall have no further duties to the seller or the purchaser regarding any disclosures required under the Residential Property Condition Disclosure Act. A real estate licensee who has not complied with the requirements of subsections A, B and C of this section shall be subject to disciplinary action by the Oklahoma Real Estate Commission as set forth in paragraph 6 of Section 858-208 of Title 59 of the Oklahoma Statutes.

E.   Real estate licensee has no duty to the seller or the purchaser to conduct an independent inspection of the property and has no duty to independently verify the accuracy or completeness of any statement made by the seller in the disclaimer statement or the disclosure statement and any amendment.

Section 837. Remedies

A.   The purchaser may recover in a civil action only in the event of any of the following:
   1.   The failure of the seller to provide to the purchaser a disclaimer statement or a disclosure statement and any amendment prior to acceptance of an offer to purchase;
   2.   The failure of the seller to disclose in the disclosure statement or any amendment provided to the purchaser a defect which was actually known to the seller prior to acceptance of an offer to purchase; or
   3.   The failure of the real estate licensee to disclose to the purchaser any defects in the property actually known to the real estate licensee prior to acceptance of an offer to purchase and which were not included in the disclosure statement or any amendment provided to the purchaser.
B.   The sole and exclusive civil remedy at common law or otherwise for a failure under subsection A of this section by the seller or the real estate licensee shall be an action for actual damages, including the cost of repairing the defect suffered by the purchaser as a result of a defect existing in the property as of the date of acceptance by the seller of an offer to purchase and shall not include the remedy of exemplary damages.
C.   Any action brought under this act shall be commenced within two (2) years after the date of transfer of real property subject to this act.
D.   In any civil action brought under this act, the prevailing party shall be allowed court costs and a reasonable attorney fee to be set by the court and to be collected as costs.
E.   A transfer of a possessory interest in property subject to this act may not be invalidated solely because of the failure of any person to comply with this act.
F.   This act applies to, regulates and determines rights, duties, obligations and remedies at common law or otherwise of the seller, the real estate licensee and the purchaser with respect to disclosure of defects in property and supplants and abrogates all common law liability, rights, duties, obligations and remedies therefore.

Section 838, Exemptions from application of act

A.   This act does not apply to:
   1.   Transfers pursuant to court order, including, but not limited to, transfers pursuant to a writ of execution, transfers by eminent domain and transfers pursuant to an order for partition;
   2.   Transfers to a mortgagee by a mortgagor or successor in interest who is in default, transfers by any foreclosure sale after default in an obligation secured by a mortgage, transfers by a mortgagee's sale under a power of sale after default in an obligation secured by any instrument containing a power of sale, or transfers by a

mortgagee who has acquired the real property at a sale conducted pursuant to a power of sale or a sale pursuant to a decree of foreclosure or has acquired the real property by deed in lieu of foreclosure;

3. Transfers by a fiduciary who is not an owner occupant of the subject property in the course of the administration of a decedent's estate, guardianship, conservatorship or trust;

4. Transfers from one co-owner to one or more other co-owners;

5. Transfers made to a spouse, or to the person or persons in the lineal line of consanguinity of one or more of the owners;

6. Transfers between spouses resulting from a decree of dissolution of marriage or a decree of legal separation or from a property settlement agreement incidental to such a decree;

7. Transfers made pursuant to mergers and from a subsidiary to a parent or the reverse;

8. Transfers or exchanges to or from any governmental entity; or

9. Transfers of a newly constructed, previously unoccupied dwelling.

B. Nothing in this act shall be construed to alter or change the requirements of Section 858-513 of Title 59 of the Oklahoma Statutes, regarding psychologically impacted real estate.

Section 839, Notices and acknowledgements

Any notices or acknowledgements required under this act need not be sworn to, verified or acknowledged.

DISCLOSURE VS. DISCLAIMER

Note that the terms *Residential Property Condition Disclosure Statement* and *Residential Property Condition Disclaimer Statement* look and sound almost identical. The one page "disclaimer" is used only when the seller has never occupied the property, has no actual knowledge of any defect, and therefore makes no disclosures concerning the condition of the property.

Otherwise, the three page "disclosure" statement is utilized to communicate known defects from the seller to the buyer.

APPENDIX A. RESIDENTIAL PROPERTY CONDITION DISCLOSURE STATEMENT

Notice to Seller: Oklahoma Law (the "Residential Property Condition Disclosure Act," Title 60, O.S., Sections 831 et.seq., effective July 1, 1995) requires Sellers of 1 and/or 2 residential dwelling units to complete this form. A Seller must complete, sign and date this disclosure form and deliver it or cause it to be delivered to a Purchaser as soon as practicable, but in any event no later than before an offer is accepted by the Seller. If the Seller becomes aware of a defect after delivery of this statement, but before the Seller accepts an offer to purchase, the Seller must deliver or cause to be delivered an amended disclosure statement disclosing the newly discovered defect to the Purchaser. If the disclosure form or amendment is delivered to a Purchaser after an offer to purchase has been made by the Purchaser, the offer to purchase shall be accepted by the Seller only after a Purchaser has acknowledged receipt of this statement and confirmed the offer to purchase in writing.

Notice to Purchaser: The declarations and information contained in this disclosure statement are not warranties, express or implied of any kind, and are not a substitute for any inspections or warranties the purchaser may wish to obtain. The information contained in this disclosure statement is not intended to be a part of any contract between the Purchaser and Seller. The information and statements contained in this disclosure statement are declarations and representations of the Seller and are not the representations of the real estate licensee.

Instructions to the Seller: (1) Answer ALL questions. (2) Report known conditions affecting the property. (3) Complete this form yourself. (4) If some items do not apply to your property, circle N/A (not applicable). If you do not know the facts, circle Unk (unknown). (5) The date of completion by you may not be more than 180 days prior to the date this form is received by a purchaser.

LOCATION OF SUBJECT PROPERTY: _____

_____

SELLER IS ___ IS NOT ___ OCCUPYING THE SUBJECT PROPERTY.

Appliances/Systems/Services: (The items below are in **NORMAL** working order)

	Circle below					Circle below		
Sprinkler System	N/A	Yes	No	Unk	Humidifier	N/A	Yes	No	Unk
Swimming Pool	N/A	Yes	No	Unk	Gas Supply __Public __Propane __Butane	N/A	Yes	No	Unk
Hot Tub/Spa	N/A	Yes	No	Unk					
Water Heater __Electric __Gas __Solar	N/A	Yes	No	Unk	Propane Tank __Leased __Owned	N/A	Yes	No	Unk
Water Purifier	N/A	Yes	No	Unk	Ceiling Fans	N/A	Yes	No	Unk
Water Softener __Leased __Owned	N/A	Yes	No	Unk	Electric Air Purifier	N/A	Yes	No	Unk
Sump Pump	N/A	Yes	No	Unk	Garage Door Opener/ Control	N/A	Yes	No	Unk
Plumbing	N/A	Yes	No	Unk	Intercom	N/A	Yes	No	Unk
Whirlpool Tub	N/A	Yes	No	Unk	Central Vacuum	N/A	Yes	No	Unk
Sewer System __Public __Septic __Lagoon	N/A	Yes	No	Unk	Security System __Rent __Own __Monitored	N/A	Yes	No	Unk
Air Conditioning					Smoke Detectors	N/A	Yes	No	Unk
System __Electric __Gas __Heat Pump	N/A	Yes	No	Unk	Dishwasher	N/A	Yes	No	Unk
					Electrical Wiring	N/A	Yes	No	Unk
Window Air Conditioner(s)	N/A	Yes	No	Unk	Garbage Disposal	N/A	Yes	No	Unk
					Gas Grill	N/A	Yes	No	Unk
Attic Fan	N/A	Yes	No	Unk	Vent Hood	N/A	Yes	No	Unk
Fireplaces	N/A	Yes	No	Unk	Microwave Oven	N/A	Yes	No	Unk
Heating System __Electric __Gas __Heat Pump	N/A	Yes	No	Unk	Built-in Oven/Range	N/A	Yes	No	Unk
					Kitchen Stove	N/A	Yes	No	Unk
					Trash Compactor	N/A	Yes	No	Unk

Seller's Initials_____ Seller's Initials_____

Buyer's Initials_____ Buyer's Initials _____

(OREC-7/12)

Page 1 of 3

LOCATION OF SUBJECT PROPERTY _____

Source of Household Water	Other Items _____	☐Yes	☐No	☐Unk
	Other _____	☐Yes	☐No	☐Unk
___Public ___Private ___Well ☐Yes ☐No ☐Unk	Other _____	☐Yes	☐No	☐Unk

IF YOU HAVE ANSWERED NO to any of the above, please explain. Attach additional pages with your signature(s).

_____
_____

		Circle below	
Zoning, Flood and Water			
1. Property is zoned: *(Check one)* ___residential ___commercial ___historical ___agricultural ___industrial ___office ___urban conservation ___other ___unknown			
2. What is the flood zone status of the property? _____			☐Unk
3. Are you aware of any flood insurance requirements concerning the property?	☐Yes	☐No	☐Unk
4. Do you have flood insurance on the property?	☐Yes	☐No	☐Unk
5. Has the property been damaged or affected by flood, storm run-off, sewer backup, drainage or grading problems?	☐Yes	☐No	☐Unk
6. Are you aware of any surface or ground water drainage systems which assist in draining the property, e.g. french drains?	☐Yes	☐No	☐Unk
7. Has there been any occurrence of water in the heating and air conditioning duct system?	☐Yes	☐No	☐Unk
8. Are you aware of water seepage, leakage or other drainage problems in any of the improvements on the property?	☐Yes	☐No	☐Unk
Additions/Alterations/Repairs			
9. Have any additions or alterations been made without required permits?	☐Yes	☐No	☐Unk
10. Are you aware of previous foundation repairs?	☐Yes	☐No	☐Unk
11. Are you aware of any alterations or repairs having been made to correct defects or problems?	☐Yes	☐No	☐Unk
12. Are you aware of any defect or condition affecting the interior or exterior walls, ceilings, slab/foundation, basement/storm cellar, floors, windows, doors, fences or garage?	☐Yes	☐No	☐Unk
13. Has the roof ever been repaired or replaced during your ownership of the property?	☐Yes	☐No	☐Unk
14. Approximate age of roof covering, if known _____ number of layers, if known _____			☐Unk
15. Do you know of any current problems with the roof?	☐Yes	☐No	☐Unk
16. Are you aware of treatment for termite or wood-destroying organism infestation?	☐Yes	☐No	☐Unk
17. Do you have a termite bait system installed on the property?	☐Yes	☐No	☐Unk
18. If yes, is it monitored by a licensed exterminating company? *(Check one)* ___yes ___no Annual cost $_____			
19. Are you aware of any damage caused by termites or wood-destroying organisms?	☐Yes	☐No	☐Unk
20. Are you aware of major fire, tornado, hail, earthquake or wind damage?	☐Yes	☐No	☐Unk
21. Are you aware of problems pertaining to sewer, septic, lateral lines or aerobic system?	☐Yes	☐No	☐Unk
Environmental			
22. Are you aware of the presence of asbestos?	☐Yes	☐No	☐Unk
23. Are you aware of the presence of radon gas?	☐Yes	☐No	☐Unk
24. Have you tested for radon gas?	☐Yes	☐No	☐Unk
25. Are you aware of the presence of lead-based paint?	☐Yes	☐No	☐Unk
26. Have you tested for lead-based paint?	☐Yes	☐No	☐Unk
27. Are you aware of any underground storage tanks on the property?	☐Yes	☐No	☐Unk
28. Are you aware of the presence of a landfill on the property?	☐Yes	☐No	☐Unk
29. Are you aware of existence of hazardous or regulated materials and other conditions having an environmental impact?	☐Yes	☐No	☐Unk
30. Are you aware of existence of prior manufacturing of methamphetamine?	☐Yes	☐No	☐Unk
31. Have you had the property inspected for mold?	☐Yes	☐No	☐Unk
32. Have you had any remedial treatment for mold on the property?	☐Yes	☐No	☐Unk
33. Are you aware of any condition on the property that would impair the health or safety of the occupants?	☐Yes	☐No	☐Unk
Property Shared in Common, Easements, Homeowner's Association, Legal			
34. Are you aware of features of the property shared in common with adjoining landowners, such as fences, driveways, and roads whose use or responsibility has an affect on the property?	☐Yes	☐No	☐Unk
35. Other than utility easements serving the property, are you aware of easements or right-of-ways affecting the property?	☐Yes	☐No	☐Unk

Seller's Initials_____ Seller's Initials_____   Buyer's Initials_____ Buyer's Initials_____

LOCATION OF SUBJECT PROPERTY _____

36. Are you aware of encroachments affecting the property?	Yes	No	Unk
37. Are you aware of a mandatory homeowner's association?	Yes	No	Unk

Amount of dues $ _____ Special Assessment $ _____
Payable: **(Check one)** ___monthly ___quarterly ___annually
Are there unpaid dues or assessments for the Property? **(Check one)** ___yes ___no
If yes, amount $ _____ Manager's Name: _____
Phone No. _____

38. Are you aware of any zoning, building code or setback requirement violations?	Yes	No	Unk
39. Are you aware of any notices from any government or government-sponsored agencies or any other entities affecting the property?	Yes	No	Unk
40. Are you aware of any filed litigation or lawsuit(s), directly or indirectly, affecting the property, including a foreclosure?	Yes	No	Unk
41. Is the property located in a fire district which requires payment?	Yes	No	Unk

Amount of fees $ _____ To Whom Paid _____
Payable **(Check one)** __monthly __quarterly __annually

42. Is the property located in a private utility district?	Yes	No	Unk

(Check applicable) water___ garbage___ sewer___ other___
If other, explain: _____
Initial membership fee $_____ annual membership fee $_____
(If more than one (1) utility, attach additional pages.)

Miscellaneous

43. Are you aware of other defect(s), affecting the property, not disclosed above?	Yes	No	Unk
44. Are you aware of any other fees or dues required on the property that you have not disclosed?	Yes	No	Unk

If you answered "YES" to any of the items 1-44 above, list the item number(s) and explain. *(If needed, attach additional pages, with your signature(s), date(s) and location of subject property.*

_____

_____

On the date this form is signed, the seller states that based on seller's **CURRENT ACTUAL KNOWLEDGE** of the property, the information contained above is true and accurate.

Are there any additional pages attached to this disclosure *(circle one)*: Yes No. If yes, how many? _____

_____   _____
Seller's Signature   Date   Seller's Signature   Date

A real estate licensee has no duty to the Seller or the Purchaser to conduct an independent inspection of the property and has no duty to independently verify the accuracy or completeness of any statement made by the seller in this disclosure statement.

The Purchaser understands that the disclosures given by the Seller on this statement is not a warranty of condition. The Purchaser is urged to carefully inspect the property and, if desired, to have the property inspected by a licensed expert. For specific uses, restrictions and flood zone status, contact the local planning, zoning and/or engineering department. The Purchaser acknowledges that the Purchaser has read and received a signed copy of this statement. This completed acknowledgement should accompany an offer to purchase on the property identified. This is to advise that this disclosure statement is not valid after 180 days from the date completed by the Seller.

_____   _____
Purchaser's Signature   Date   Purchaser's Signature   Date

The disclosure and disclaimer statement forms and the Oklahoma Residential Property Condition Disclosure Act information pamphlet are made available at the Oklahoma Real Estate Commission (OREC), Denver N. Davison Building, 1915 N. Stiles, Suite 200, Oklahoma City, Oklahoma 73105, or visit OREC's Web site www.orec.ok.gov.

(OREC-7/12)   Page 3 of 3

APPENDIX B. RESIDENTIAL PROPERTY CONDITION DISCLAIMER STATEMENT FORM

Seller instructions: Oklahoma Law (the "Residential Property Condition Disclosure Act," 60, O.S. Section 831 et. seq., effective July 1, 1995) **requires a seller** of 1 and 2 residential dwelling units **to deliver, or cause to be delivered, a disclaimer statement to a purchaser as soon as practicable, but in any event before acceptance of an offer to purchase if you, the seller: 1) have never occupied the property and make no disclosures** concerning the condition of the property; <u>and</u> **2) have no actual knowledge of any defect** concerning the property.

If, however, you occupied the property or know of a defect in regard to the property, you must complete and deliver, or cause to be delivered, a "Residential Property Condition Disclosure Statement" to the purchaser.

Also, if you become aware of a defect <u>after</u> delivery of this disclaimer statement to a purchaser, but before you accept an offer to purchase, you must complete and deliver, or cause to be delivered, a "Residential Property Condition Disclosure Statement" to a purchaser.

Completion of this form by you **may not be more than 180 days prior to the date this form is received by a purchaser.**

Note: If this disclaimer statement **is delivered to a purchaser after an offer to purchase has been made by the purchaser,** the offer to purchase **shall be accepted by you only after** a purchaser has acknowledged receipt of this statement and confirmed the offer to purchase.

> Defect means a condition, malfunction, or problem that would have a materially adverse effect on the monetary value of the property, or that would impair the health or safety of future occupants of the property.

(For more information on the requirements of the law, please refer to the Residential Property Condition Disclosure Information Pamphlet.)

Seller's Disclaimer Statement

The undersigned seller states that seller has <u>never</u> occupied the property located at _____
_____, Oklahoma; makes <u>no</u> disclosures concerning the condition of the property; AND has <u>no</u> actual knowledge of any defect.

_____ _____ _____ _____
Seller's Signature   Date   Seller's Signature   Date

Purchaser's Acknowledgment

The purchaser shall sign and date this acknowledgment. The purchaser is urged to carefully inspect the subject property and, if desired, to have the property inspected by an expert. The purchaser acknowledges that purchaser has read and received a signed copy of this statement. This completed acknowledgement should accompany an offer to purchase you make on the property identified above.

_____ _____ _____ _____
Purchaser's Signature   Date   Purchaser's Signature   Date

Note to seller and purchaser: A real estate licensee has no duty to the seller or purchaser to conduct an independent inspection of the property and has no duty to independently verify the accuracy or completeness of any statement made by the seller in this disclaimer statement.

The disclosure and disclaimer statement forms and the Residential Property Condition Disclosure Information Pamphlet are made available by the Oklahoma Real Estate Commission, 2401 NW 23rd St, Suite 18, Oklahoma City, Oklahoma 73107-2431, or visit OREC's Web site www.orec.state.ok.us

(OREC-7/03)

CHAPTER 4:
Residential Property Condition Disclosure Statement;
Residential Property Condition Disclaimer Statement
End of Chapter Quiz

1. The Oklahoma *Residential Property Condition Disclosure Act* requires:

   a. sellers of one or two residential dwelling units to comply.
   b. the *Residential Property Condition Disclosure Statement to be delivered to the* purchaser *as soon as practicable.*
   c. the *Residential Property Condition Disclosure Statement to be delivered to the* purchaser *no later than before an offer is accepted by the seller.*
   d. all of these

2. The entity responsible for developing and amending the disclosure and disclaimer forms pertaining to the Act and making such forms available is the:

   a. attorney general.
   b. Real Estate Commission.
   c. Oklahoma Association of REALTORS®.
   d. state legislature.

3. The disclosure statement must include:

   a. an identification of items and improvements which are included in the sale of the property and whether such items or improvements are in normal working order.
   b. a statement of whether the seller has actual knowledge of defects with structural and mechanical systems as well as land use matters, to name a few.
   c. a statement that the information and statements contained in the disclosure statement are declarations and representations of the seller and are not the representations of the real estate licensee.
   d. all of these

4. The seller is not liable for:

   a. a defect or other condition if it was disclosed in the disclosure statement.
   b. information which was not within the actual knowledge of the seller.
   c. the delivery by a public agency of any information required to be disclosed by the seller of the property.
   d. all of these

5. Remedies available to a prevailing purchaser for failure by the seller or the real estate licensee to comply with the Act include:

   a. three times the cost of repairing the defect suffered by the purchaser.
   b. to bring civil action within three years after the date of transfer for discovery of the defect(s).
   c. the award of court costs and reasonable attorney fees.
   d. all of these

Chapter 5

Broker Operational Procedures

This chapter addresses many of the requirements of the broker in Oklahoma such as regulations regarding the place of business, the law of agency, the maintenance of trust accounts, and the Oklahoma Fair Housing Law.

DO YOU KNOW???

Do you know the regulations pertaining to the broker's place of business such as physical facility and signage requirements?

Are you familiar with the mandatory obligations of the broker to *all* parties in a transaction?

Can you name some of the events that will lead to the termination of an agency relationship?

Have you been acquainted with rules regarding the handling of earnest money deposits?

Do you know about the Oklahoma Fair Housing Law?

These are just some of the topics to be covered in this chapter.

BROKER REQUIREMENTS

Please note there are additional operational requirements of Brokers in subchapter 9 of section 605.

Place of Business – §858-310 requires every real estate broker to maintain a specific place of business that is in compliance with all local laws and is available to the public during reasonable business hours. Brokers may open branch offices and a branch office license must be obtained for each additional location. Every office must be supervised by a separate broker and who is considered a *managing broker* of the office. The broker may supervise the main office. A broker may be the broker for more than one firm provided the firms are at the same location. Brokers are charged with the duty of supervision of all associates as well as unlicensed and licensed assistants.

Brokers must maintain a place of business consisting of at least one enclosed room or building of stationary construction wherein negotiations and closing of real estate transactions of others may be conducted and carried on with privacy and wherein the broker's books, records and files pertaining to real estate transactions of others are maintained. The office may be in the residence of the broker.

Brokerage offices must have a sign, on or about the entrance of the office, which shall be easily observed and read by persons about to enter. Each sign shall contain the name of the broker or trade name registered with the Commission, and if a partnership, association or corporation, shall contain the name or trade name of such firm. The sign must indicate that the party is a real estate broker and not a private party, to include, but not limited to,

BUFFALO REALTY, INC.
(918) 555-1212
Harriet Smith
Licensed Real Estate Broker

"company", "realty", or "real estate", as the case may be, all in letters not less than one (1) inch in height. Legal abbreviations following the trade name or name under which the broker is licensed shall be acceptable as long as they are easily identifiable by the public.

Each licensed broker or entity must register in writing to the Commission all trade names used prior to the trade name being advertised or displayed and the broker must notify the Commission in writing of all deleted or unused trade names.

In the event of the death, disability, retirement or cessation of employment for any reason by the designated branch office broker, and the branch office is to continue to do business, the main office broker shall appoint a new branch office broker and file the appropriate documents with the Commission within ten (10) days of the occurrence of the event.

Licensing requirements of business entities such as partnerships and corporation are spelled out, beginning with 605:10-7-8.

Duties to the Parties – Section §858-353 defines the duties and responsibilities to parties in a transaction. The following list represents the mandatory obligations of the broker to *all* parties in a transaction (may not be waived):

- Treat all parties with honesty and exercise reasonable skill and care;
- Unless specifically waived in writing by a party to the transaction:
    - receive all written offers and counteroffers,
    - reduce offers or counteroffers to a written form upon request of any party to a transaction, and
    - present timely all written offers and counteroffers;
- Timely account for all money and property received by the broker,
- Keep confidential information received from a party or prospective party confidential. The confidential information shall not be disclosed by a firm without the consent of the party disclosing the information unless consent to the disclosure is granted in writing by the party or prospective party disclosing the information, the disclosure is required by law, or the information is made public or becomes public as the result of actions from a source other than the firm.
    - The following information shall be considered confidential and shall be the only information considered confidential in a transaction:
        - that a party or prospective party is willing to pay more or accept less than what is being offered,
        - that a party or prospective party is willing to agree to financing terms that are different from those offered,
        - the motivating factors of the party or prospective party purchasing, selling, leasing, optioning or exchanging the property,
        - and information specifically designated as confidential by a party unless such information is public;

- Disclose information pertaining to the property as required by the Residential Property Condition Disclosure Act;
- Comply with all requirements of The Oklahoma Real Estate License Code and all applicable statutes and rules.

The following list represents the mandatory obligations of the broker to the party for whom the broker is *providing brokerage services* (also may not be waived):

- Inform the party in writing when an offer is made that the party will be expected to pay certain costs, brokerage service costs and approximate amount of the costs; and
- Keep the party informed regarding the transaction.

When working with both parties to a transaction, such as in a dual agency relationship, these mandatory obligations are due to both parties in the transaction.

Broker associates, sales associates, and provisional sales associates should note that these duties to the parties extend to them as well as agents of the broker. These three categories of licensees must be associated with a real estate broker and may not enter into a brokerage agreement with a party in the associate's name and are only permitted to enter into the agreement in the name of the broker.

Brokerage Agreements – All brokerage agreements, listing agreements and buyer representation contracts, must include the duties and responsibilities set forth in Section 858-353 above. A broker who is providing brokerage services to one or both parties shall describe and disclose in writing these duties before the parties sign a contract to sell, purchase, lease, option, or exchange real estate.

Should the brokerage provide services to both parties in the same transaction, the broker is responsible to provide written notice, to both parties, that the firm is providing brokerage services to both parties. This disclosure must be made prior to the parties signing a contract to purchase, lease, option or exchange real estate.

Termination of Agency – Upon the termination, expiration, or completion of performance in an agency relationship, the broker owes no further duties or responsibilities to the party after except:

- to account for all monies and property relating to the transaction; and
- to keep confidential all confidential information received by the broker during the broker's relationship with a party.
- any provisions specified in the brokerage agreement

Note that the payment of commission by either party to the broker does not determine the agency relationship with that party.

§858-303B might seem out of place in the midst of the 300 section pertaining to requirements for licensure. These items pertains to an accounting of expenditure for services for any real estate broker who charges and collects any fees in advance of the services provided by the broker. It requires the broker to provide a detailed accounting of expenditures to the client within ten (10) days after the time specified to perform such services or upon written request from the client, but no longer than one (1) year from date of contract for such services.

BROKER TRUST ACCOUNTS

Not all states require the broker to maintain a trust account. A broker usually has the option of depositing funds collected from clients into a Commission-regulated trust account or to never take funds and have earnest money deposits, as an example, made payable to the title company and turn the funds over to that company. An Oklahoma broker is not required to maintain a trust or escrow account unless monies or other items belonging to others are accepted.

Examples of funds we are referring to include earnest money deposits, rents and security deposits, and money advanced by a client for the payment of expenses.

605:10-13-1 lists the requirements and rules pertaining to a broker who maintains a trust account:

(A)   The broker shall deposit all checks and monies of whatever kind and nature belonging to others in a separate account in a financial institution wherein the deposits are insured by an agency of the federal government.

(B)   The broker is required to be a signor on the account.

(C)   The account must be in the name of the broker as it appears on the license or trade name as registered with the Commission and styled as a trust or escrow account and shall be maintained by the broker as a depository for deposits belonging to others.

(D)   All escrow funds shall be deposited before the end of the third banking day following acceptance of an offer by an offeree unless otherwise agreed to in writing by all interested parties.

(E)   The broker shall maintain such funds in said account until the transaction involved is consummated or terminated and proper accounting made.

(F)   The broker shall at all times, maintain an accurate and detailed record thereof.

Commingling – As defined in an earlier chapter, "commingling" is the mixing of the broker's funds with the funds held in trust for another. We also defined *conversion* is actually spending or using those funds for the broker's own use. Commingling and conversion are two areas where many brokers have found themselves knee-deep in trouble with the Commission and disciplined accordingly. Brokers are required to keep accurate records and must carefully account for trust funds. A broker may not keep any personal funds in the trust account except amounts sufficient to insure the integrity of the account and cover any charges made by the financial institution for servicing the trust or escrow account.

Oklahoma allows the broker to place escrow monies in an interest bearing account provided the broker discloses, in writing to all parties, that the account bears interest and the party receiving the interest is named. The Commission does not prohibit the broker from receiving the earned interest.

Brokers are required to notify the Commission in writing of all trust or escrow accounts, security deposit accounts, rental management operating accounts, and interest bearing accounts in which trust funds are held and inform the Commission in writing of any accounts which are closed and no longer in use.

A broker shall pay over all sums of money held promptly after the closing of the transaction. In the event a transaction does not consummate, the broker shall promptly disburse the trust funds to the proper party in accordance with the terms of the contract. In the event a dispute arises pertaining to the disbursement, the broker shall follow rule 605:10-13-3 or may file an interpleader action with the appropriate court.

605:10-13-3 states that in the event of a dispute regarding the disbursement of any monies or other valuables held by a broker in escrow, the broker shall continue to retain said money or valuables in escrow until he or she has a written release from all parties consenting to its disposition or until a civil action is filed to determine its disposition at which time he or she may pay or turn it in to the court.

605:10-13-2 defines the duty of an associate to remit monies, valuable documents and other property coming into his or her possession. The associate:

(1) shall turn over all documents, files and monies deposited, payments made, or things of value received by the associate to his or her broker *promptly*; and
(2) Shall deliver a copy of all instruments to any party or parties executing the same when such has been prepared by the associate or pertains to the consummation of a transaction in which he or she participated.

While maintaining a trust account, the broker must use a reliable bookkeeping system which accounts for canceled checks, check book, deposit receipts, general accounts ledger, etc. which will accurately and clearly disclose full compliance with the law relating to the maintaining of trust accounts.

> *An Oklahoma broker must maintain all records and files for a minimum of*
> *five (5) years after consummation or termination of a transaction.*

Brokers are permitted to store files and records on *alternative media*. Alternative media is defined as media that uses an electronic device to store or retrieve the information on any computer technology. Trust account records must be maintained by the broker in their original format for a minimum of two (2) years and then transferred to an alternative media. All other records, with the exception of trust account records, may be transferred at any time to an alternative media. Yet, still, all records must be maintained for a minimum of five years.

OKLAHOMA FAIR HOUSING LAW

Oklahoma has adopted its own Oklahoma Fair Housing Law Under the jurisdiction of the Human Rights Commission and was updated through July 2007. As many states have also done, Oklahoma's Fair Housing Law mirrors federal legislation regarding discrimination outlined earlier in this textbook. The law identifies unlawful discriminatory housing practices such as to refuse to sell or rent to any person because of race, color, religion, gender, national origin, age, familial status, or handicap. Similar to the federal law, it also identifies the exemptions. Article 5 references the Human Rights Commission and identifies the body's powers of enforcement including the complaint and hearing processes.

To vindicate the public interest, the Human Rights Commission may assess a civil penalty against the respondent in an amount that does not exceed $10,000 if the respondent has been adjudged by order of the Commission or a court to have committed a prior discriminatory housing practice; or $25,000 if the respondent has been adjudged by order of the Commission or a court to have committed one other discriminatory housing practice during the last five-year period. $50,000 if two or more discriminatory housing practices during the prior seven-year period. The Attorney General may file a civil action in district court for appropriate relief with even stiffer penalties.

The entire body of law pertaining to the Oklahoma Fair Housing Law can be found within Title 25, Article 4A, Section 1451 through Article 5 Section 1508.

CHAPTER 5:
Broker Operational Procedures
End of Chapter Quiz

1. Regulations pertaining to the signage of a brokerage office include:

   a. There must be a sign, on or about the entrance of the office, which is easily observed and read.
   b. Each sign must contain the name of the brokerage as registered with the Commission.
   c. Signs contain letters not less than one inch in height.
   d. all of these

2. Upon the expiration of an agency relationship, the broker owes no further duties or responsibilities to the party after except:

   a. to account for all monies and property relating to the transaction.
   b. to keep confidential all confidential information received by the broker.
   c. any provisions specified in the brokerage agreement.
   d. all of these

3. Regulations pertaining to trust accounts in Oklahoma include:

   a. Monies shall be maintained in a separate account within a financial institution that is federally insured.
   b. The sales associate is required to be a signor on the account.
   c. All escrow funds shall be deposited before the end of the second banking day following acceptance of an offer.
   d. all of these

4. The wrongful act of actually spending or using trust funds for the broker's own use is called:

   a. commingling.
   b. coercion.
   c. conversion.
   d. misrepresentation.

5. After the consummation or termination of a transaction, the Oklahoma broker must maintain all records and files for a minimum of:

   a. three years.
   b. five years.
   c. seven years.
   d. ten years.

OKLAHOMA REAL ESTATE COMMISSION

This is a legally binding Contract; if not understood seek advice from an attorney.

ACKNOWLEDGMENT AND CONFIRMATION OF DISCLOSURES

Prior to entering into Contract, the following items (as applicable) have been disclosed and/or delivered and hereby confirmed:

Buyer acknowledges and confirms that the Broker providing brokerage services to the Buyer has described and disclosed their duties and responsibilities to the Buyer prior to the Buyer signing this Contract.

☐ **(Applicable for in-house transactions only)** Buyer acknowledges and confirms that the broker is providing brokerage services to both parties to the transaction prior to the parties signing this Contract.

Buyer acknowledges receipt of Residential Property Condition Disclosure or Disclaimer Form (as applicable to residential real property improved with not less than one nor more than two dwelling units) pursuant to Title 60 O.S., Section 831-839:

☐ Buyer has received a Residential Property Condition Disclosure Statement Form (completed and signed by the Seller) and dated within 180 days of receipt.

☐ Buyer has received a Residential Property Condition Disclaimer Statement Form (completed and signed by the Seller) and dated within 180 days of receipt.

☐ This transaction is exempt from disclosure requirements pursuant to Title 60, O.S., Section 838.

☐ Disclosure not required under the Residential Property Condition Disclosure Act.

Buyer acknowledges receipt of Lead-Based Paint/Hazards Disclosures with Appropriate Acknowledgment (if property constructed before 1978)

☐ Buyer has signed the "Disclosure of Information on Lead-Based Paint and Lead-Based Paint Hazards" form, which has been signed and dated by Seller and applicable Licensee(s), and has also received a copy of the Lead-Based Paint Pamphlet titled "Protect Your Family From Lead in Your Home."

☐ Property was constructed in 1978 or thereafter and is exempt from this disclosure.

☐ The subject of this transaction is not a residential dwelling and does not require a disclosure on Lead-Based Paint/ Hazards.

Buyer acknowledges and confirms the above and further, Buyer acknowledges receipt of Estimate of Costs associated with this transaction and acknowledges that a Contract Information Booklet has been made available to the Buyer in print, or at www.orec.ok.gov.

Buyer Name (Printed): _____   Buyer Name (Printed): _____

Buyer Signature: _____   Buyer Signature: _____

Dated: _____   Dated: _____

Seller acknowledges and confirms that the Broker providing brokerage services to the Seller has described and disclosed their duties and responsibilities to the Seller prior to the Seller signing this Contract.

☐ **(Applicable for in-house transactions only)** Seller acknowledges and confirms that the broker is providing brokerage services to both parties to the transaction prior to the parties signing this Contract.

Seller further acknowledges receipt of Estimate of Costs associated with this transaction and that a Contract Information Booklet has been made available to the Seller in print, or at www.orec.ok.gov.

Seller Name (Printed): _____   Seller Name (Printed): _____

Seller Signature: _____   Seller Signature: _____

Dated: _____   Dated: _____

This form was created by the Oklahoma Real Estate Contract Form Committee and approved by the Oklahoma Real Estate Commission.

OREC CONFIRMATION OF DISCLOSURES (11-2013)   Page 1 of 1

85

Property Address _____

OKLAHOMA REAL ESTATE COMMISSION
This is a legally binding Contract; if not understood seek advice from an attorney.

OKLAHOMA UNIFORM CONTRACT OF SALE OF REAL ESTATE
RESIDENTIAL SALE

CONTRACT DOCUMENTS. The Contract is defined as this document with the following attachment(s):
(check as applicable)

____ Conventional Loan   ____ Single Family Mandatory Homeowners' Association
____ FHA Loan   ____ Condominium Association
____ VA Loan   ____ Townhouse Association
____ Assumption   ____ Supplement
____ Seller Financing   ____ Sale of Buyer's Property - Presently Under Contract
                                ____ Sale of Buyer's Property - Not Under Contract
____ _____

PARTIES. THE CONTRACT is entered into between:

_____"Seller"

and _____ "Buyer".

The Parties' signatures at the end of the Contract, which includes any attachments or documents incorporated by reference, with delivery to their respective Brokers, if applicable, will create a valid and binding Contract, which sets forth their complete understanding of the terms of the Contract. This agreement shall be binding upon and inure to the benefit of the parties hereto and their respective heirs, successors and permitted assigns. The Contract shall be executed by original signatures of the parties or by signatures as reflected on separate identical Contract counterparts (carbon, photo, fax or other electronic copy). The parties agree that as to all aspects of this transaction involving documents an electronic signature shall have the same force and effect as an original signature pursuant to the provisions of the Uniform Electronic Transactions Act, 12A, Oklahoma Statutes, Section 15-101 et seq. All prior verbal or written negotiations, representations and agreements are superceded by the Contract, which may only be modified or assigned by a further written agreement of Buyer and Seller.

The parties agree that all notices and documents provided for in this contract shall be delivered to the parties or their respective brokers, if applicable. Seller agrees to sell and convey by General Warranty Deed, and Buyer agrees to accept such deed and buy the Property described herein, on the following terms and conditions:

The Property shall consist of the following described real estate located in _____ County, Oklahoma.

1. **LEGAL DESCRIPTION.** _____

_____

_____

_____

Property Address   City   Zip

Together with all fixtures and improvements, and all appurtenances, subject to existing zoning ordinances, plat or deed restrictions, utility easements serving the Property, **including** all mineral rights owned by Seller, which may be subject to lease, unless expressly reserved by Seller in the Contract and **excluding** mineral rights previously reserved or conveyed of record (collectively referred to as "the Property.")

2. **PURCHASE PRICE, EARNEST MONEY AND SOURCE OF FUNDS.** This is a CASH TRANSACTION unless a Financing Supplement is attached. The Purchase Price is $_____ payable by Buyer as follows: Buyer has paid $_____ as Earnest Money on execution of the Contract, and Buyer shall pay the balance of the purchase price and Buyer's Closing costs at Closing. Upon execution of the Contract, the Earnest Money shall be deposited in the trust account of _____ or if left blank, the Listing Broker's trust account, as part payment of the purchase price and/or closing costs. If interest accrues on Earnest Money Deposit in Listing Broker's trust account, said interest shall be paid to "Oklahoma Housing Foundation."

3. **CLOSING, FUNDING AND POSSESSION.** The Closing process includes execution of documents, delivery of deed and receipt of funds by Seller and shall be completed on or before _____, ("Closing Date") or not later than _____ days (five [5] days if left blank) thereafter caused by a delay of the Closing process, or such later date as may be necessary in the Title Evidence Paragraph of the Contract. Possession shall be transferred upon conclusion of Closing process unless otherwise provided below:

_____

In addition to costs and expenses otherwise required to be paid in accordance with terms of the Contract, Buyer shall pay Buyer's Closing fee, Buyer's recording fees, and all other expenses required from Buyer. Seller shall pay documentary stamps required, Seller's Closing fee, Seller's recording fees, if any, and all other expenses required from Seller. Funds required from Buyer and Seller at Closing shall be cash, cashier's check, wire transfer, or as determined by the provider of settlement services.

This form was created by the Oklahoma Real Estate Contract Form Committee and approved by the Oklahoma Real Estate Commission.

Property Address _____

4. ACCESSORIES, EQUIPMENT AND SYSTEMS. The following items, if existing on the Property, unless otherwise excluded, shall remain with the Property at no additional cost to Buyer:

- Attic and ceiling fan(s)
- Bathroom mirror(s)
- Other mirrors, if attached
- Central vacuum & attachments
- Floor coverings, if attached
- Key(s) to the property
- Built-in and under cabinet/counter appliance(s)
- Free standing slide-in/drop-in kitchen stove
- Built-in sound system(s)/speaker(s)
- Lighting & light fixtures
- Fire, smoke and security system(s), if owned
- Shelving, if attached

- Fireplace inserts, logs, grates, doors and screens
- Free standing heating unit(s)
- Humidifier(s), if attached
- Water conditioning systems, if owned
- Window treatments & coverings, interior & exterior
- Storm windows, screens & storm doors
- Garage door opener(s) & remote transmitting unit(s)
- Fences (includes sub-surface electric & components)
- Mailboxes/Flag poles
- Outside cooking unit(s), if attached
- Propane tank(s) if owned

- TV antennas/satellite dish system(s) and control(s), if owned
- Sprinkler systems & control(s)
- Swimming Pool/Spa equipment/ accessories
- Attached recreational equipment
- Exterior landscaping and lighting
- Entry gate control(s)
- Water meter, sewer/trash membership, if owned
- All remote controls, if applicable
- Transferable Service Agreements and Product Warranties

A. Additional Inclusions. The following items shall also remain with the Property at no additional cost to Buyer:

_____
_____

B. Exclusions. The following items shall not remain with the Property: _____

_____.

5. TIME PERIODS SPECIFIED IN CONTRACT. Time periods for Investigations, Inspections and Reviews and Financing Supplement shall commence on _____ **(Time Reference Date)**, regardless of the date the Contract is signed by Buyer and Seller. The day after the Time Reference Date shall be counted as day one (1). If left blank, the Time Reference Date shall be the third day after the last date of signatures of the parties.

6. RESIDENTIAL PROPERTY CONDITION DISCLOSURE. No representations by Seller regarding the condition of Property or environmental hazards are expressed or implied, other than as specified in the Oklahoma Residential Property Condition Disclosure Statement ("Disclosure Statement") or the Oklahoma Property Condition Disclaimer Statement ("Disclaimer Statement"), if applicable. A real estate licensee has no duty to Seller or Buyer to conduct an independent inspection of the Property and has no duty to independently verify accuracy or completeness of any statement made by Seller in the Disclosure Statement and any amendment or the Disclaimer Statement.

7. INVESTIGATIONS, INSPECTIONS and REVIEWS.

A. Buyer shall have _____ days (10 days if left blank) after the Time Reference Date to complete any investigations, inspections, and reviews. Seller shall have water, gas and electricity turned on and serving the Property for Buyer's inspections, and through the date of possession or Closing, whichever occurs first. If required by ordinance, Seller, or Seller's Broker, if applicable, shall deliver to Buyer, in care of Buyer's Broker, if applicable, within five (5) days after the Time Reference Date any written notices affecting the Property.

B. Buyer, together with persons deemed qualified by Buyer and at Buyer's expense, shall have the right to enter upon the Property to conduct any and all investigations, inspections, and reviews of the Property. Buyer's right to enter upon the Property shall extend to Oklahoma licensed Home Inspectors and licensed architects for purposes of performing a home inspection. Buyer's right to enter upon the Property shall also extend to registered professional engineers, professional craftsman and/or other individuals retained by Buyer to perform a limited or specialized investigation, inspection or review of the Property pursuant to a license or registration from the appropriate State licensing board, commission or department. Finally, Buyer's right to enter upon the Property shall extend to any other person representing Buyer to conduct an investigation, inspection and/or review which is lawful but otherwise unregulated or unlicensed under Oklahoma Law. Buyer's investigations, inspections, and reviews may include, but not be limited to, the following:

1) **Disclosure Statement or Disclaimer Statement unless exempt**
2) **Flood, Storm Run off Water, Storm Sewer Backup or Water History**
3) **Psychologically Impacted Property and Megan's Law**
4) **Hazard Insurance** (Property insurability)
5) **Environmental Risks**, including, but not limited to soil, air, water, hydrocarbon, chemical, carbon, asbestos, mold, radon gas, lead-based paint
6) **Roof**, structural members, roof decking, coverings and related components
7) **Home Inspection**
8) **Structural Inspection**
9) **Fixtures, Equipment and Systems Inspection.** All fixtures, equipment and systems relating to plumbing (including sewer/septic system and water supply), heating, cooling, electrical, built-in appliances, swimming pool, spa, sprinkler systems, and security systems
10) **Termites and other Wood Destroying Insects Inspection**

This form was created by the Oklahoma Real Estate Contract Form Committee and approved by the Oklahoma Real Estate Commission.

11) **Use of Property.** Property use restrictions, building restrictions, easements, restrictive covenants, zoning ordinances and regulations, mandatory Homeowner Associations and dues

12) **Square Footage.** Buyer shall not rely on any quoted square footage and shall have the right to measure the Property.

13) _____

C. TREATMENTS, REPAIRS AND REPLACEMENTS (TRR).

1) **TERMITE TREATMENTS AND OTHER WOOD DESTROYING INSECTS.** Seller's obligation to pay treatment and repair cost in relation to termites and other wood destroying insects shall be limited to the residential structure, garage(s) and other structures as designated in Paragraph 13 of the Contract and as provided in subparagraph C2b below.

2) **TREATMENTS, REPAIRS, REPLACEMENTS AND REVIEWS.** Buyer or Buyer's Broker, if applicable, within 24 hours after expiration of the time period referenced in Paragraph 7A of the Contract, shall deliver to Seller, in care of the Seller's Broker, if applicable, a copy of all written reports obtained by Buyer, if any, pertaining to the Property and Buyer shall select one of the following:

   a. If, in the sole opinion of the Buyer, results of Investigations, Inspections or Reviews are unsatisfactory, the Buyer may cancel the Contract by delivering written notice of cancellation to Seller, in care of Seller's Broker, if applicable, and receive refund of Earnest Money.

   OR

   b. Buyer, upon completion of all Investigations, Inspections and Reviews, waives Buyer's right to cancel as provided in 7C2a above, by delivering to Seller, in care of Seller's Broker, if applicable, a written list on a Notice of Treatments, Repairs, and Replacements form (TRR form) of those items to be treated, repaired or replaced (including repairs caused by termites and other wood destroying insects) that are not in normal working order (defined as the system or component functions without defect for the primary purpose and manner for which it was installed. Defect means a condition, malfunction or problem, which is not decorative, that will have a materially adverse effect on the value of a system or component).

      i. Seller shall have _____ days (5 days if blank) after receipt of the completed TRR form from Seller's Broker, if applicable, to obtain costs estimates. Seller agrees to pay up to $_____ ("Repair Cap") of costs of TRR's. If Seller, or Seller's Broker, if applicable, obtains cost estimates which exceed Repair Cap, Seller, or Seller's Broker, if applicable, shall notify Buyer or Buyer's Broker, if applicable, in writing, within two days after receipt of cost estimates.

      If the amount of the TRR's exceed the amount of the Repair Cap, Buyer and Seller shall have _____ days (3 days if blank) thereafter to negotiate the payment of costs in excess of Repair Cap. If a written agreement is reached, Seller shall complete all agreed TRR's prior to the Closing Date. If an agreement is not reached within the time specified in this provision, the Contract shall become null and void and Earnest Money returned to Buyer.

      ii. If Seller fails to obtain cost estimates within the stated time, Buyer shall then have _____ days (5 days if blank) to:

         a) Enter upon the Property to obtain costs estimates and require Seller to be responsible for all TRR's as noted on Buyer's TRR form, up to the Repair Cap; and,

         b) If the amount of the TRR's exceed the amount of the Repair Cap, Buyer and Seller shall have _____ days (3 days if blank) thereafter to negotiate the payment of costs in excess of Repair Cap. If a written agreement is reached, Seller shall complete all agreed TRR's prior to the Closing Date. If an agreement is not reached within the time specified in this provision, the Contract shall become null and void and Earnest Money returned to Buyer.

D. EXPIRATION OF BUYER'S RIGHT TO CANCEL CONTRACT.

1) Failure of Buyer to complete one of the following shall constitute acceptance of the Property regardless of its condition:
   a. Perform any Investigations, Inspections or Reviews;
   b. Deliver a written list on a TRR form of items to be treated, repaired and replaced; or
   c. Cancel the Contract within the time periods in Investigations, Inspections or Reviews Paragraph.

2) After expiration of the time periods in Investigations, Inspections and Reviews Paragraph, Buyer's inability to obtain a loan based on unavailability of hazard insurance coverage shall not relieve the Buyer of the obligation to close transaction.

3) After expiration of the time periods in Investigations, Inspections and Reviews Paragraph, any square footage calculation of the dwelling, including but not limited to appraisal or survey, indicating more or less than quoted, shall not relieve the Buyer of the obligation to close this transaction.

This form was created by the Oklahoma Real Estate Contract Form Committee and approved by the Oklahoma Real Estate Commission.

OREC RESIDENTIAL SALES (11-2013)   Page 3 of 6

88

Property Address _____

E. INSPECTION OF TREATMENTS, REPAIRS AND REPLACEMENTS AND FINAL WALK-THROUGH.
   1) Buyer, or other persons Buyer deems qualified, may perform re-inspections of Property pertaining to Treatments, Repairs and Replacements.
   2) Buyer may perform a final walk-through inspection, which Seller may attend. Seller shall deliver Property in the same condition as it was on the date upon which Contract was signed by Buyer (ordinary wear and tear excepted) subject to Treatments, Repairs and Replacements.
   3) All inspections and re-inspections shall be paid by Buyer, unless prohibited by mortgage lender.

8. **RISK OF LOSS.** Until transfer of Title or transfer of possession, risk of loss to the Property, ordinary wear and tear excepted, shall be upon Seller; after transfer of Title or transfer of possession, risk of loss shall be upon Buyer. (Parties are advised to address insurance coverage regarding transfer of possession prior to Closing.)

9. **ACCEPTANCE OF PROPERTY.** Buyer, upon accepting Title or transfer of possession of the Property, shall be deemed to have accepted the Property in its then condition. No warranties, expressed or implied, by Sellers, Brokers and/or their associated licensees, with reference to the condition of the Property, shall be deemed to survive the Closing.

10. **TITLE EVIDENCE.**

   A. BUYER'S EXPENSE. Buyer, at Buyer's expense, shall obtain:
   (Check one)
   ☐ **Attorney's Title Opinion**, which is not rendered for Title Insurance purposes.
       OR
   ☐ **Commitment for Issuance of a Title Insurance Policy** based on an Attorney's Title Opinion which is rendered for Title Insurance purposes for the Owner's and Lender's Title Insurance Policy.

   B. SELLER'S EXPENSE. Seller, at Seller's expense, within thirty (30) days prior to Closing Date, agrees to make available to Buyer the following (*collectively referred to as "the Title Evidence"*):
   1) A complete surface-rights-only Abstract of Title, last certified to a date subsequent to the Time Reference Date, by an Oklahoma licensed and bonded abstract company;
       OR
       A copy of Seller's existing owner's title insurance policy issued by a title insurer licensed in the State of Oklahoma together with a supplement surface-rights-only abstract last certified to a date subsequent to the Time Reference Date, by an Oklahoma licensed and bonded abstract company;
   2) A current Uniform Commercial Code Search Certificate; and
   3) An inspection certificate (commonly referred to as a "Mortgage Inspection Certificate") prepared subsequent to the Time Reference Date by a licensed surveyor, which shall include a representation of the boundaries of the Property (without pin stakes) and the improvements thereon.

   C. LAND OR BOUNDARY SURVEY. By initialing this space _____, Buyer agrees to waive Seller's obligation to provide a Mortgage Inspection Certificate. Seller agrees that Buyer, at Buyer's expense, may have a licensed surveyor enter upon the Property to perform a Land or Boundary (Pin Stake) Survey, in lieu of a Mortgage Inspection Certificate, that shall then be considered as part of the Title Evidence.

   D. BUYER TO EXAMINE TITLE EVIDENCE.
   1) Buyer shall have ten (10) days after receipt to examine the Title Evidence and to deliver Buyer's objections to Title to Seller or Seller's Broker, if applicable. In the event the Title Evidence is not made available to Buyer within ten (10) days prior to Closing Date, said Closing Date shall be extended to allow Buyer the ten (10) days from receipt to examine the Title Evidence.
   2) Buyer agrees to accept title subject to: (i) utility easements serving the property, (ii) building and use restrictions of record, (iii) set back and building lines, (iv) zoning regulations, and (v) reserved and severed mineral rights, which shall not be considered objections for requirements of Title.

   E. SELLER TO CORRECT ISSUES WITH TITLE (IF APPLICABLE), POSSIBLE CLOSING DELAY. Upon receipt by Seller, or in care of Seller's Broker, if applicable, of any title requirements reflected in an Attorney's Title Opinion or Title Insurance Commitment, based upon the standard of marketable title set out in the Title Examination Standards of the Oklahoma Bar Association, the parties agree to the following:

   1) Seller, at Seller's expense, shall make reasonable efforts to obtain and/or execute all documents necessary to cure title requirements identified by Buyer; and
   2) Delay Closing Date for _____ days [thirty (30) days if blank], or a longer period as may be agreed upon in writing, to allow Seller to cure Buyer's title requirements. In the event Seller cures Buyer's objection prior to the delayed Closing Date, Buyer and Seller agree to close within five (5) days of notice of such cure. In the event that title requirements are not cured within the time specified in this subparagraph, the Buyer may cancel the Contract and receive a refund of Earnest Money.

This form was created by the Oklahoma Real Estate Contract Form Committee and approved by the Oklahoma Real Estate Commission.

OREC RESIDENTIAL SALES (11-2013)   Page 4 of 6

89

F. Upon Closing, any existing Abstract(s) of Title, owned by Seller, shall become the property of Buyer.

11. **TAXES, ASSESSMENTS AND PRORATIONS.**

A. General ad valorem taxes for the current calendar year shall be prorated through the date of closing, if certified. However, if the amount of such taxes has not been fixed, the proration shall be based upon the rate of levy for the previous calendar year and the most current assessed value available at the time of Closing.

B. The following items shall be paid by Seller at Closing: (i) Documentary Stamps; (ii) all utility bills, actual or estimated; (iii) all taxes other than general ad valorem taxes which are or may become a lien against the Property; (iv) any labor, materials, or other expenses related to the Property, incurred prior to Closing which is or may become a lien against the Property.

C. At Closing all leases, if any, shall be assigned to Buyer and security deposits, if any, shall be transferred to Buyer. Prepaid rent and lease payments shall be prorated through the date of Closing.

D. If applicable, membership and meters in utility districts to include, but not limited to, water, sewer, ambulance, fire, garbage, shall be transferred at no cost to Buyer at Closing.

E. If the property is subject to a mandatory Homeowner's Association, dues and assessments, if any, based on most recent assessment, shall be prorated through the date of Closing.

F. All governmental and municipal special assessments against the property (matured or not matured), not to include Homeowner's Association special assessments, whether or not payable in installments, shall be paid in full by Seller at Closing.

12. **RESIDENTIAL SERVICE AGREEMENT.**

(CHECK ONE)

A. ☐ The Property shall not be covered by a Residential Service Agreement.

B. ☐ Seller currently has a Residential Service Agreement in effect on the Property. Seller, at Seller's expense, shall transfer the agreement with one (1) year coverage to the Buyer at Closing.

C. ☐ The Property shall be covered by a Residential Service Agreement selected by the Buyer at an approximate cost of $_____. Seller agrees to pay $_____ and Buyer agrees to pay the balance.

The Seller and Buyer acknowledge that the real estate broker(s) may receive a fee for services provided in connection with the Residential Service Agreement.

Buyer acknowledges that a Residential Service Agreement does not replace/substitute Property inspection rights.

13. **ADDITIONAL PROVISIONS.**

_____
_____
_____
_____

14. **MEDIATION.** Any dispute arising with respect to the Contract shall first be submitted to a dispute resolution mediation system servicing the area in which the Property is located. Any settlement agreement shall be binding. In the event an agreement is not reached, the parties may pursue legal remedies as provided by the Contract.

15. **BREACH AND FAILURE TO CLOSE.**

A. **UPON BREACH BY SELLER.** If the Buyer performs all of the obligations of Buyer, and if, within five (5) days after the date specified for Closing under Paragraph 3 of the Contract, Seller fails to convey the Title or fails to perform any other obligations of the Seller under this Contract, then Buyer shall be entitled to either cancel and terminate this Contract, return the abstract to Seller and receive a refund of the Earnest Money, or pursue any other remedy available at law or in equity, including specific performance.

B. **UPON BREACH BY BUYER.** If, after the Seller has performed Seller's obligation under this Contract, and if, within five (5) days after the date specified for Closing under Paragraph 3 of the Contract, the Buyer fails to provide funding, or to perform any other obligations of the Buyer under this Contract, then the Seller may, at Seller's option, cancel and terminate this Contract and retain all sums paid by the Buyer, but not to exceed 5% of the purchase price, as liquidated damages, or pursue any other remedy available at law or in equity, including specific performance.

16. **INCURRED EXPENSES AND RELEASE OF EARNEST MONEY.**

A. **INCURRED EXPENSES.** Buyer and Seller agree that any expenses, incurred on their behalf, shall be paid by the party incurring such expenses and shall not be paid from Earnest Money.

This form was created by the Oklahoma Real Estate Contract Form Committee and approved by the Oklahoma Real Estate Commission.

Property Address _____

B. RELEASE OF EARNEST MONEY. In the event a dispute arises prior to the release of Earnest Money held in escrow, the escrow holder shall retain said Earnest Money until one of the following occur:

1) A written release is executed by Buyer and Seller agreeing to its disbursement;
2) Agreement of disbursement is reached through Mediation;
3) Interpleader or legal action is filed, at which time the Earnest Money shall be deposited with the Court Clerk; **or**
4) The passage of thirty (30) days from the date of final termination of the Contract has occurred and options 1), 2) or 3) above have not been exercised; Broker escrow holder, at Broker's discretion, may disburse Earnest Money. Such disbursement may be made only after fifteen (15) days written notice to Buyer and Seller at their last known address stating the escrow holder's proposed disbursement.

17. **DELIVERY OF ACCEPTANCE OF OFFER OR COUNTEROFFER.** The Buyer and Seller authorize their respective Brokers, if applicable, to receive delivery of an accepted offer or counteroffer.

18. **NON-FOREIGN SELLER.** Seller represents that at the time of acceptance of this contract and at the time of Closing, Seller is not a "foreign person" as such term is defined in the Foreign Investments in Real Property Tax Act of 1980 (26 USC Section 1445(f) et. Sec) ("FIRPTA"). If either the sales price of the property exceeds $300,000.00 or the buyer does not intend to use the property as a primary residence then, at the Closing, and as a condition thereto, Seller shall furnish to Buyer an affidavit, in a form and substance acceptable to Buyer, signed under penalty of perjury containing Seller's United States Social Security and/or taxpayer identification numbers and a declaration to the effect that Seller is not a foreign person within the meaning of Section "FIRPTA."

19. **EXECUTION BY PARTIES.**

AGREED TO BY BUYER:

On This Date_____

_____
Buyer's Printed Name

_____
Buyer's Signature

_____
Buyer's Printed Name

_____
Buyer's Signature

AGREED TO BY SELLER:

On This Date_____

_____
Seller's Printed Name

_____
Seller's Signature

_____
Seller's Printed Name

_____
Seller's Signature

TERMINATION OF OFFER. The above Offer shall automatically terminate on _____ **at 5:00 p.m.,** unless withdrawn prior to acceptance or termination.

OFFER REJECTED AND SELLER IS NOT MAKING A COUNTEROFFER _____ _____, 20_____

_____
Seller's Signature

_____
Seller's Signature

EARNEST MONEY RECEIPT AND INSTRUCTIONS

Receipt of $_____ ☐ Check ☐ Cash as Earnest Money Deposit, to be deposited in accordance with the terms and conditions of <u>PURCHASE PRICE, EARNEST MONEY, AND SOURCE OF FUNDS Paragraph.</u> Broker(s) acknowledges receipt of Earnest Money and Listing Broker, if applicable, shall deposit said funds in accordance with Paragraph 2 of this Contract. If deposited in an escrow account other than the Listing Broker, the Listing Broker, if applicable, shall provide a copy of receipt to the Selling Broker.

_____
Date   Selling Broker/Associate Signature

_____
(Print Name) Selling Broker/Associate

_____
Company Name

_____
Address   Phone

_____
Date   Listing Broker/Associate Signature

_____
(Print Name) Listing Broker/Associate

_____
Company Name

_____
Address   Phone

This form was created by the Oklahoma Real Estate Contract Form Committee and approved by the Oklahoma Real Estate Commission.

Appendix A

Answer Keys to
End of Chapter Quizzes

OKLAHOMA SPECIFIC QUIZZES

Chapter 1

1. C
2. D
3. B
4. A
5. B
6. B
7. D
8. B
9. D
10. D
11. A
12. D
13. D
14. D
15. D
16. A
17. B
18. C
19. D
20. B

Chapter 2

1. D
2. C
3. C
4. C
5. A

Chapter 3

1. D
2. B
3. B
4. C
5. D
6. A
7. A
8. B
9. B
10. D

Chapter 4

1. D
2. B
3. D
4. D
5. C

Chapter 5

1. D
2. D
3. A
4. C
5. B

CPSIA information can be obtained at www.ICGtesting.com
Printed in the USA
LVOW09s1622010416

481786LV00024B/652/P